D1189993

AMERICANA LIBRARY

ROBERT E. BURKE, EDITOR

Men of Destiny

BY

WALTER LIPPMANN

INTRODUCTION BY RICHARD LOWITT

DRAWINGS BY ROLLIN KIRBY

UNIVERSITY OF WASHINGTON PRESS

SEATTLE AND LONDON

ACKNOWLEDGMENT

I AM grateful to the editors of the *Atlantic Monthly, Foreign Affairs, Harper's Magazine,* the *New Republic,* the *Saturday Review of Literature, Vanity Fair,* and the *Yale Review* for their courteous permission to reprint, with slight revision, some of the papers contained in this volume.

W. L.

New York, May 10, 1927.

CONTENTS

INTRODUCTION

Men of Destiny is not one of Walter Lippmann's
better known works, perhaps because it is less philosophical than most of them. In this volume Lippmann
is more the editor viewing current developments
than the political philosopher speculating on them in
an effort to probe new directions or to expand on possible consequences. It is this side of Lippmann, that
of a journalist, that has received relatively little attention from scholars.

Lippmann's first book, *A Preface to Politics,* was
published in 1913, less than three years after his
graduation from Harvard, where he was a brilliant
student, president of the Harvard Socialist Club,
and George Santayana's assistant in a philosophy
course. In this book and in *Drift and Mastery,* published the following year, Lippmann, not yet having
celebrated his twenty-fifth birthday, sought to clarify
the role of the intellectual in introducing plan and
purpose into society while seeking to overcome both
the complexity of the material and "the prejudices

of the public." Creative leadership, as Lippmann envisioned it in these volumes, would have "much less use for lawyers and a great deal more for scientists." It would seek the services of philosophers and social engineers who could make society conscious of its problems and especially of its purposes.

During the Wilson era, Lippmann had an opportunity to put his ideas into practice, first as an editor of the *New Republic* and then during the war years as an expert collaborating with statesmen: as a special assistant to Secretary of War Newton D. Baker and as secretary to the collection of experts known as the Inquiry, organized by Colonel E. M. House to begin planning the peace. He also served in Military Intelligence in France, and the war's end found him in Paris where he observed peacemaking while working with Colonel House. He returned to the United States disillusioned about the failure of Versailles and the lack of information most citizens had about the peace conference.

The "Red Scare" of 1919 and the election of Warren G. Harding the following year increased his concern about the inadequacy of public information and the ability of powerful officials, such as Attorney-General A. Mitchell Palmer, to manipulate and suppress it with the idea of gaining power to control and direct public opinion. Though he moved from the *New Republic* in 1924 to the more rough and tumble journalism of the *New York World*, his books during these years concerned themselves with the problem of the adequacy of public information and the use of public opinion in overcoming the confusion and apathy so characteristic of the Harding years. The most important of these volumes, *Public Opinion,* published in 1922, reflected Lippmann's departure from his earlier belief in a rational social order, as did its successor *The Phantom Public,* published in 1925. Not only were facts complex and obscure but the ability to perceive and assess them was limited by ignorance, emotion, distortion, tradition, stereotypes, and manipulation as well. Only a handful of "insiders" had the ability to penetrate this maze, and Lippmann suggested that it was now the role of the intellectual to serve this policy-making group. The intellectual, who in Lippmann's earlier works was to play a predominant role in molding a more rational social order, a decade later was merely to present necessary factual data to a ruling elite who would use this information as it saw fit. Thus by the time Lippmann published *Men of Destiny* his progressive optimism had yielded to skepticism; his belief in reason had crumbled before his increased awareness of the force of the irrational in human behavior; and his faith in democracy was being supplanted by an interest in an elite capable of making rational decisions.

Within this context, with his social thought in a state of flux, Lippmann published *Men of Destiny* in 1927. It consisted of eighteen essays, some of which were reprinted with slight revisions from periodicals. The majority focused on individuals prominent dur-

ing the twenties; others were concerned with issues
or ideas that aroused the interest of the American
people. While the emphasis was on the politics and
diplomacy of the period, it was not exclusively so.
Though not all of the essays were concerned with
men of destiny and their problems in the decade of
the 1920's, and though they, inevitably, vary in merit,
the volume still provides one of the best introductions
to that all-important and ever-interesting decade of
Republican ascendancy. Rollin Kirby, cartoonist for
the *New York World* and one of the best practition-
ers of this difficult but fascinating art at the time,
provided a sketch to introduce each essay.

In a preface to *A Modern Reader,* a series of arti-
cles "on present day life and culture" published a
decade later with a college audience in mind, the
editors Allan Nevins and Walter Lippmann observed:

For the present-day world is confused, complex,
challenging beyond all precedent. It changes with bewildering rapidity; it contains forces that are as baf-
fling as they are powerful. It is no longer compart-
mentalized as it once seemed to be; economics and
politics are more and more inextricably commingled,
science alters the primary postulates of both, and
letters and art mirror social changes and new scientific and philosophical concepts with marvelous
celerity. . . .

This statement, as these essays reveal, could have applied to the twenties as indeed to almost any period of our history. Nevertheless, it does suggest that in his efforts to understand and analyze politics on both the national and international scene Lippmann's focus and the questions he asked of his limited data were cast on a broad and challenging canvas. Thus, without the benefit of perspective and without access to primary sources which are available in many instances to scholars today, *Men of Destiny* still has something to say to readers forty years after its publication. The interpretations and insights it presents are in attune with recent scholarship. Indeed, the volume anticipated modern scholarship in that Lippmann saw "the new urban civilization" pushing forward toward the center of national affairs and threatening, for better or for worse, "that older American civilization of town and country." At the very vortex of this conflict between the new immigrants seeking positions of prominence in American life and citizens of older ethnic stocks caught in a "conflict between the tradition which Americans have professed and the tradition upon which they really intend to act" was Alfred E. Smith.

Similarly, Lippmann's brief analysis of Calvin Coolidge gets at the essence of his popularity. Increasing numbers of native-born Americans appreciated a President who expounded the old virtues they knew and practiced while growing up in small-town or rural America but which seemingly had little rele-

vance to their hectic and increasingly complicated
lives in an urbanized and industrialized society. Lippmann's essays on William E. Borah, devoted primarily to the Senator as chairman of the Committee on
Foreign Relations and his support of the proposal
for the "outlawry of war," are harshly critical and in
accord with the view of modern scholars, many of
whom stress the failure of statesmen to provide enforcement procedures in the campaign to renounce
war as an instrument of national policy. Borah, he
observed, by "affirming the oldest American traditions and the simplest popular prejudices" sought to
"thwart evil by publicity" and built his career on opposition. Sharp words. But recent scholars carefully
examining the voluminous collection of Borah papers
in the Library of Congress have not reached mark-
edly different conclusions.

Another example of his astute analysis can be
found in his review of "Notes on Democracy."
Though he had doubts himself, Lippmann pierces
the biting irony and quickly gets to the heart of
H. L. Mencken's elitism and antidemocratic criticism, something that caught the attention of most
observers at least a decade later. In this essay he
seeks to answer the question, "Why Henry L.
Mencken is as popular as he is in a country in which
he professes to dislike most of the population." And
so it goes, whether he is discussing political indifference, Sinclair Lewis, censorship, foreign policy, or
Warren G. Harding, writing without the benefit of

hindsight and with a journalist's knowledge of current events, which usually is not as accurate or as complete as a historian's, Lippmann has provocative and meaningful points to make and insights to present to readers four decades later, who only now are beginning to comprehend the 1920's in historical perspective.

He acutely observed that progressivism persevered in the twenties particularly in the farming states "where the new surplus of wealth was not available, and where in consequence the old progressive motives and traditions survived." Elsewhere the feeling of prosperity "robbed progressive idealism of its urgency," while the expounders of the "New Capitalism" accepted many of the attitudes its predecessors "would have thought was tommyrot." They were "more enlightened" and would take "ever so much more trouble to please." Though progressivism and the new capitalism involved special segments of the population, the masses of the people were aroused by questions that engaged their emotions, and here Lippmann mentioned prohibition, the Ku Klux Klan, Romanism, fundamentalism, and immigration rather than those that aroused the progressive mind: tariff, taxation, credit, and corporation control. Prohibition, the Ku Klux Klan, fundamentalism, and xenophobia, Lippmann regarded as extreme but authentic expressions of the outlook "of the older American village civilization making its last stand" against "the deepening of that breach of tradition which invariably accompany the development of a metropolitan civilization."

He also came to grips with the question of why rural America opposed cities and within this context viewed the campaign to forbid the teaching of Darwinism as an attempt to stem the tide of the metropolitan spirit "threatening to dissolve the mores of village civilization." And in his provocative essay on William Jennings Bryan, Lippmann again anticipated modern scholarship. He argued that the Bryan of the Scopes trial in 1925 was no different than "the leader of the hosts of progress in 1896." In both instances Bryan was insisting on the rights of the majority and popular rule. In the course of his exegesis Lippmann clearly dislodged the notion of inconsistency in Bryan's later years, a view many scholars only recently have come to accept. Lippmann also saw further evidence of urban-rural tension in the controversy over the Eighteenth Amendment, which he regarded as an attempt to impose the moral ideals of the village upon the whole nation. And in politics this tension helped explain why "our political leaders are greatly occupied in dampening down interest, in obscuring issues, and in attempting to distract attention from the realities of American life."

In the realm of foreign policy Lippmann again expressed views which students of the period have further probed and developed. In these essays he suggested the ironic contradiction between seeking to outlaw war on the one hand and Secretary of State

Frank Kellogg's policy of attempting to guarantee American vested rights against social progress as the peoples of Latin America conceived it. And in a most perspicacious discussion of American empire in the Caribbean, Lippmann made the telling point that the Caribbean countries were "dealt with absent-mindedly, in a left-handed way, without realization of the responsibilities involved" by State Department officials who were far from specialists in the area or country of their concern, a point still in need of historical examination at the present time. In short, Lippmann's analysis, of which the above is only a sparse outline, could pass muster in any graduate seminar or college classroom today. It raised points that more recent studies have further developed; others still need examination. All, however, are relevant to the more penetrating questions scholars are asking about the 1920's now that they are able to secure some perspective on the decade.

The brief essay on Harding, for example, was written in 1920 and is entitled "An Anticipation of Harding." In it Lippmann made a prediction of considerable accuracy when he wrote: "The Grand Dukes have chosen their weak Tsar in order to increase the power of the Grand Dukes." Its validity was already evident by 1927 and probably explains why he chose to include it in the volume. Yet Lippmann with greater subtlety compared Harding to William Jennings Bryan, the spokesman of rural America, and perhaps unwittingly suggested Harding's appeal and significance for the modern student when he commented on the belief of both men in the "simple faith that any deserving fellow can do anything." In the framework of an industrialized and urbanized America, where technical training of sorts was becoming a prerequisite for earning a livelihood and where machinery soon would begin to displace men in certain industries on a noticeable scale, this statement is probably more meaningful than his accurate prediction of the shenanigans of the "Ohio Gang" in Washington, D.C. It indicates Harding's appeal to an older America, and not to a nation that was in the process of transforming itself.

What makes his account so fresh and so modern is that Lippmann tried to take people and events seriously. Consequently he avoided the ballyhoo, hoopla, and jazz age approach that characterized so many contemporary accounts of the decade. This approach was usually followed either by nostalgic views or by debunking details and cynical caricaturing that distorted the decade out of clear focus to serve ulterior purposes, such as reminding readers in the depression-ridden decade of the thirties that things were simpler and much more fun in that previous era of wonderful nonsense. Other authors sought to impress on their readers that the retreat from responsibility on the part of national leaders in the twenties played a major role in bringing on the crises that befell the United States in the following decades. To be sure, both of these views contain a segment of truth, but they are not the whole picture. Recent scholarship seeks to understand the 1920's in terms of its own problems and is only now beginning to explore fully the dimensions of the traumatic tensions that beset a nation which, as the census of 1920 revealed, was predominantly urbanized and industrialized.

Walter Lippmann sensed these tensions and attempted to diagnose them. These brief and incisive essays provide an excellent introduction for the modern reader seeking an understanding of this much misunderstood period in our history. As Lippmann and Allan Nevins remarked in the preface referred to above: "If students are not given some acquaintance with the newer issues, the newer problems, and the most important of the new arguments, they will feel very bewildered indeed when they walk out into the glare and clamor of the world."

More so than any other contemporary volume and well in advance of modern scholarship, *Men of Destiny* sought to tell it as it was during the 1920's. More or less ignoring the foibles and the follies of the twenties, the aspect that is all too often examined, Lippmann in *Men of Destiny* suggested the aches and agonies of a nation backing into the twentieth century. It is less controversial than his other important works because it is primarily analytical and professes no remedies for resolving difficulties facing the American people and their leaders, either in the form of older doctrines or modern theories. Nevertheless, these essays contain many of the classic themes Lipp-

mann has continued to grapple with: the rule of the
majority and the rights of the minority, the balancing
of liberty and authority, individual freedom and the
power of the state, pressure groups versus the public interest, isolationism and internationalism, the
"phantom public" and the "omnipotent citizen," and,
as an earlier volume stated it, "Drift and Mastery."
In *Men of Destiny* the themes are suggested within
the context of the 1920's, and they add more to our
comprehension of that decade than to an understanding of Walter Lippmann.

Though at the time this volume was published
Lippmann was serving as the editor of a partisan
Democratic newspaper, the *New York World,* his
politics are not evident from a reading of *Men of
Destiny.* He was criticizing and analyzing to provide
understanding and not to take sides. More than half
of the essays deal with political and hence partisan
topics, but they generate the light of understanding
and avoid the heat of partisanship. Unlike most of
his other important books, these essays reveal Lippmann as a political thinker speaking in specific more
so than in general terms about ethical and social
problems. Because of his great ability and insight derived from a rich and informed background as political philosopher, public servant, author, and editor,
Walter Lippmann was able to view the current problems and long-range issues evident in the 1920's in an
analytical and judicious rather than in an active and
partisan way. And in doing so, he produced a book

which, more than four decades after it first appeared, still serves as an excellent introduction to any reader seeking an understanding of the 1920's.

RICHARD LOWITT

Lexington, Kentucky
October, 1968

MEN OF DESTINY

AL SMITH: A MAN OF DESTINY

RECENTLY New York celebrated another of Al Smith's triumphs. Yet the cheering was not altogether light-hearted, for this time even the deaf could hear the rumble of thunder in the distance which grows louder and more threatening the more victories he wins. It is impossible any longer to ignore the signs of an impending fate. For with each new proof of his power in New York the tension throughout the country becomes more ominous. His victories have ceased to be victories merely; they are premonitions. When he wins nowadays he does not merely survive a Democratic disaster, or bend a hostile legislature to his will, or defeat a power like Hearst's. These victories, which prove his mettle and increase his stature, cast long shadows ahead of them. They have come to portend a tragic conflict in which he seems destined to be the central figure.

I call it tragic not because it is bound to end in misery, but because the forces at work are beyond the control of the human will. One cannot say that the new urban civilization which is pushing Al Smith forward into national affairs is better or worse than that older American civilization of town and country which dreads him and will resist him. But one can say that they do not understand each other, and that neither has yet learned that to live it must let live. The conflict is the inevitable consequence of our history. It seems, however, to be the fate of this genial man to deepen that conflict and to hasten it, and to make us face the conflict sooner than we are ready. I think this is his destiny, not because he pursues it, or perhaps even wholly understands it, but because his undeniable virtues make issues clear that have long been blurred and postponed.

Governor Smith is the first man of the new immigration who by every professed standard of American politics is completely available as a candidate for President. The new immigrants began to come about 1850. For seventy-five years, in spite of their vast influence in local politics, they have produced nobody who could fairly be considered for the Presidency. Now from their midst has come such a man. They have put forward a man whose record in public office both as legislator and as executive is distinguished. They have produced a political manager of the first order. They have produced a vote getter who seems to possess a kind of magic. They have produced a man whom his opponents at home not only respect but like. And they have produced him in New York, which is the state above all others that the Democratic Party must win if it is to defeat the Republican Party in a straight contest.

The availability of Al Smith is glaring, indisputable, overwhelming. And yet he is unavailable. By the unspoken and unwritten law of the United States, as it stands to-day, he cannot be nominated by any national party.

Thus, because of his virtues, he brings to open issue the conflict between the tradition which Americans have professed and the tradition upon which they really intend to act. As long as there was nobody in sight among the newer immigrant people who could seriously be considered for President, the fiction could persist that all careers were open to talent, and that a man was a man for all that. It was not necessary to inquire whether the fiction was seriously meant since there was nobody to challenge it. But Al Smith does challenge it in the most downright sort of way by the sheer fact of his power and his success. His advent has seemed to mark the end of the Age of Innocence. It has put to the test our most ancient boasts, and waked us to wonder whether after all the old faith in human equality was an illusion. Are the castes and the schisms of the Old World native also to our soil? Are we after all not the New World of which we talk but the Old World extended on fresh lands? These questions hang upon the progress of Al Smith. For with him the millions of half-enfranchised Americans are making their first bid for power.

Perhaps I should say rather that they are making their first tangible bid for recognition. For Al Smith is not the leader of a political movement which seeks to impose a new policy upon the United States. He has not promised the city people who follow him a new heaven and a new earth. His people have not been promised anything, unless it be relief from the Volstead Act, and that hope of relief is only an incidental element of their devotion to him. He has no program such as the Labor Party in England offers to the unprivileged classes of England. Nor does he seem to believe that a reconstruction of American society is necessary or desirable. He is really a perfectly conservative man about property, American political institutions, and American ideals. He believes in the soundness of the established order and in the honesty of its ideals. He knows how to play according to the rules. The principal reforms he has advocated are wholly respectable; they are the reforms of Elihu Root. The brilliancy of Governor Smith's administration has not been due to its radicalism, but to a kind of supremely good-humored intelligence and practical imagination about the ordinary run of affairs. He has made his Republican opponents at Albany look silly, not because he was so progressive and they were so reactionary, but because he knew what he was doing and they did not. He is a glutton for detail and a master of it.

He is a politician who deals with persons and facts and ideas so concretely and so simply that he can preach the eternal verities without sounding stale or trite or verbose. He is what a conservative ought to be always if he knew his business. He can operate with extraordinary skill, with fine deference to expert opinion, and with a sure instinct for realities, the institutions on which most conservatives expend so much rhetoric and fear.

The essential conservatism of Governor Smith makes it difficult to conceal the actual objection to him. He cannot be attacked as an alien bent on destroying American institutions, or even as a revolutionist, like the elder LaFollette, for example, who would undermine the rights of property and the power of the courts. Al Smith is not identified with any of the radicalism which causes the American Defense Society to shiver so volubly. He is not a pacifist, and not what the more ignorant members of the Senate call an internationalist; he has no designs on the institution of matrimony, he does not read free verse, he probably never heard of Freud, and if you inquired closely you would find, I think, that he did not accept the revelation according to Darwin. He is against prohibition and for free speech, but so are Elihu Root and Nicholas Murray Butler. The worst that can be said against him politically is that he belongs to Tammany Hall, and that can't be said very fiercely or very sincerely in this generation which knows that Tammany is a political machine, no worse certainly and in some respects much better than other political machines. Al Smith, in short, would be one hundred percent except for the accident of birth.

In fact, one can go further and assert that Governor Smith is the most powerful conservative in urban America. Great cities with their violent contrasts of riches and poverty have produced class hatred the world over. They have done so in America. Politicians, of course, have sought to capitalize this hatred, and if you look at the big cities you will find in almost every one either Hearst himself or an imitator of Hearst. His henchmen represent the nearest thing to a bolshevist spirit which the comparatively benign American scene has produced.

The spirit is denatured, clownish and bereft both of the intellectual dignity of the hard dogmas of Lenin and of the personal courage which Leninism implies. It is a kind of a squalid, shuffling meanness of envy and ambition. In New York City the spokesman of this spirit was Mayor Hylan. For seven years he conducted a dull, suspicious, hysterical and foolish kind of class war. There was no power in New York that could stop him until Smith took the field. Smith alone could reach the people Hylan could reach; Smith alone could face and return the fire of the Hearst press. That he chose to do so was a supreme test of his quality. It was proof that he does not represent a barbarian uprising, but a social movement that is reputable in its own right.

He holds these crowds as no man can hold them. He holds them without the promise of a millennium, without a radical program, without appeal to their hatreds, without bribes and doles and circuses. How does he do it? It is no answer to say that he has magnetism, for then you must ask what there is about Al Smith that magnetizes the people of all the cities. The answer, I think, is that they feel he has become the incarnation of their own hope and pride; he is the man who has gone, as they would like but do not quite dare to go, out into the great world to lift from them the secret sense of inferiority. They have belonged for seventy-five years to a secondary order of citizenship. Perhaps he will breach the walls. They have been tolerated but they are not accepted. Perhaps he, who is one of them, will be accepted.

They have no particular notions about what Al Smith might do as President of the United States. But they have a very deep sense that their own self-respect depends in some measure on the admission that Al Smith might be President of the United States. It is his nomination, more than his election, which matters here. Democratic candidates are used to being defeated, and the defeat of Al Smith would not constitute a reflection upon his people. But the refusal to nominate Al Smith when, by every political test but that of race and religion, he is easily the strongest Democrat in the United States, that refusal is taken by all the newer peoples of the cities as a denial that they have been fully admitted to America. Just as the pride of the Japanese is unbearably hurt by the refusal to admit a quota of 146 Japanese a year, so the pride of the whole new population is involved now in the treatment which the Democratic Party accords to Alfred E. Smith.

And yet I should have made melodrama out of tragedy if I left the impression that the conflict is merely between liberty and intolerance, between merit and prejudice. The older American stocks in the South and the West, and in the East, too, are not all Ku Kluxers, and the Governor's more hasty friends show an intolerance when they believe that Al Smith is the victim of purely religious prejudice. Quite apart even from the sincere opposition of the prohibitionists, the objection to Tammany, the sectional objection to New York, there is an opposition to Smith which is as authentic and, it seems to me, as poignant as his support. It is inspired by the feeling that the clamorous life of the city should not be acknowledged as the American ideal.

In spite of the frantic efforts of every backwater town to make itself a bright metropolis, in spite of realtors and boosters, in spite of the mania for size and the delusions of grandeur which are known as progress, there is still an attachment to village life. The attachment is sometimes as vague as the religion preached at a liberal church forum, but it is just strong enough to justify the fear that strange and dangerous things will come out of Babylon. The cities exist, but they are still felt to be alien, and in this uncertainty as to what the cities might yield up, men turn to the old scenes from which the leaders they always trusted have come. The farmhouse at Plymouth with old Colonel Coolidge doing the chores is an inestimable part of President Coolidge's strength. The older Americans feel that in such a place as that American virtue was bred, a cool, calm, shrewd virtue, with none of the red sins of the sidewalks of New York.

That, at bottom, is the opposition to Al Smith, and not the nonsense about setting up the Pope in the East Wing of the White House. The Ku Kluxers may talk about the Pope to the lunatic fringe, but the main mass of the opposition is governed by an instinct that to accept Al Smith is to certify and sanctify a way of life that does not belong to the America they love. Here is no trivial conflict. Here are the new people, clamoring to be admitted to America, and there are the older people defending their household gods. The rise of Al Smith has made the conflict plain, and his career has come to involve a major aspect of the destiny of American civilization.

December, 1925.

CALVIN COOLIDGE: PURITANISM
DE LUXE

C. BASCOM SLEMP, who was once Secretary to the President, has recently published a book called "The Mind of the President." Most of it is an anthology of Mr. Coolidge's utterances; but the first fifteen pages were written by Mr. Slemp. They are not exactly a blinding illumination. They contain the standard eulogy which is applied to all Presidents by their loudest admirers. For the President, no matter who he is, is always like Washington and like Lincoln in one or more respects, and it transpires that Mr. Coolidge is no exception to the rule. We learn that he is also like Andrew Jackson.

As a biographical device there are great, unexploited possibilities in this method. A man might write an analysis of Jack Dempsey in terms of

Julius Caesar, Mark Antony, and Buddha. Paraphrasing Mr. Slemp he would say of Jack Dempsey that "in this respect his chief forerunner" was Julius Caesar who for a time was champion of the world. Adverting to Mr. Dempsey's private affairs he would say, "I think Jack Dempsey is like Mark Antony in this respect." In discussing the hero's disinclination to meet an opponent whom he might injure, the biographer would then compare him to Buddha who jumped into a fire in the guise of a rabbit to cook himself as a meal for a starving beggar, but first carefully shook off the fleas on his hide so as not to hurt them. Jack Dempsey could be described in this fashion, I insist, just as Mr. Coolidge can be described as combining certain of the better features of Washington, Lincoln, and Andrew Jackson.

But it is just as well to admit that in addition to the similarities there are striking differences. Washington, for example, was a rebel against constituted authority; he assisted at the creation of a government which had not existed before, and he presided over the government when it was necessary to make precedents instead of following them. Andrew Jackson led and consummated a social revolution; Lincoln fought and won a civil war. To compare Mr. Coolidge with these men is like saying that the contented captain of a houseboat on an inland river is in many respects like the captain of a ship at sea.

Mr. Coolidge may be a great captain but he has

never been to sea. He came into office after the great postwar deflation had run its course, and the postwar scandals had run theirs. He inherited a war-time system of taxation which his predecessors had had the pain of imposing. He had the delightful problem of dealing with a surplus and not a deficit, and the pleasure of reducing taxes. A foolish man might have squandered the surplus and not reduced the taxes. Mr. Coolidge took good care of the surplus. Except for the inter-Allied debts, Mr. Coolidge has fortunately not had a single problem in statesmanship of the first order to deal with. As I write it is still uncertain whether he has settled the debts; it is very certain that he has failed to convince any one in Europe that the United States is generous, although the terms of the Italian debt settlement are very generous indeed.

For the rest, he has approached but done nothing about coal, agriculture or shipping, the three domestic questions which trouble the placid waters. There is no great insistence anywhere that he do anything. These problems produce a certain amount of local inconvenience, but no widespread distress and discontent. It is not imperative that anything should be done. On the contrary, a widespread distaste of political activity is the controlling mood of public life in this country to-day.

Mr. Coolidge's genius for inactivity is developed to a very high point. It is far from being an indolent inactivity. It is a grim, determined, alert inactivity which keeps Mr. Coolidge occupied constantly. Nobody has ever worked harder at inactivity, with such force of character, with such unremitting attention to detail, with such conscientious devotion to the task. Inactivity is a political philosophy and a party program with Mr. Coolidge, and nobody should mistake his unflinching adherence to it for a soft and easy desire to let things slide. Mr. Coolidge's inactivity is not merely the absence of activity. It is on the contrary a steady application to the task of neutralizing and thwarting political activity wherever there are signs of life.

The White House is extremely sensitive to the first symptoms of any desire on the part of Congress or of the executive departments to do something, and the skill with which Mr. Coolidge can apply a wet blanket to an enthusiast is technically marvelous. There have been Presidents in our time who knew how to whip up popular enthusiasm. There has never been Mr. Coolidge's equal in the art of deflating interest. This mastery of what might be called the technique of anti-propaganda is worthy of prolonged and profound study by students of public opinion. The naïve statesmen of the pre-Coolidge era imagined that it was desirable to interest the people in their government, that public discussion was a good thing, that indignation at evil was useful. Mr. Coolidge is more sophisticated. He has discovered the value of diverting attention from the government, and with an exquisite subtlety that amounts to genius, he has used dullness and boredom as political devices.

I do not know whether Mr. Coolidge was born with this gift or whether he developed it by necessity in the absence of certain other political gifts. But I do know that in its present development it is no mean gift. The Democratic Party has good reason to know this, for the Democrats have been flabbergasted and routed by Mr. Coolidge's skill in destroying issues. The Democrats are simple folks used to heating themselves up to a terrific temperature over any issue. They only feel at peace with themselves when they are in an ecstatic broil. They simply do not know what to do with Mr. Coolidge. They hit his party an awful blow. They knocked three members out of his Cabinet and covered them with disgrace. And what happened? Did Mr. Coolidge defend his Cabinet? He did not. Did he denounce the grafters? He did not. Did he prosecute the grafters? Not very fiercely. He managed to get the public so bored that they could bear it no longer, and to make the Democrats thoroughly disliked for raising such a dull row. It was superb. To every yawp Mr. Coolidge can match a yawn. He has had the country yawning over the outcry against relieving the super-rich of taxes, yawning over Colonel Mitchell, yawning over the World Court, yawning over the coal strike. He has brought his technique to such perfection that one paper announced the conclusion of the coal strike in streamer headlines, saying "Coolidge Wins Coal Victory; Denies He Interfered."

This active inactivity suits the mood and certain of the needs of the country admirably. It suits all the business interests which want to be let alone. It suits everybody who is making money who wants to let well enough alone. And it suits all those who have become convinced that government in this country has become dangerously complicated and top-heavy, and that it is important to reduce and decentralize the Federal power. Mr. Coolidge, though a Republican, is no Hamiltonian Federalist. Mr. Slemp is right in saying that he has stopped, if not reversed, the Republican nationalizing tendency which runs from Hamilton to Roosevelt. He has just stopped it, mind you. He has not replaced it with anything. He has just stopped it while business is good.

The politicians in Washington do not like Mr. Coolidge very much, for they thrive on issues, and he destroys their business. But the people like him, not only because they like the present prosperity, and because at the moment they like political do-nothingism, but because they trust and like the plainness and nearness of Calvin Coolidge himself. This is one of the most interesting conjunctions of our age.

As a nation we have never spent so much money

on luxury and pleasure as we are spending now. There has never in all history been such a widespread pursuit of expensive pleasure by a whole people. The American people can afford luxury and they are buying it furiously, largely on the instalment plan. And in the White House they have installed a frugal little man who in his personal life is the very antithesis of the flamboyant ideal that everybody is frantically pursuing. They have not only installed him in the White House, but they trust him utterly as they hear his voice on expensive radio sets; they praise him as they ride in expensive motor cars; they toast him at banquets where there is more food than can be eaten. At a time when Puritanism as a way of life is at its lowest ebb among the people, the people are delighted with a Puritan as their national symbol.

They are delighted with the oil lamps in the farmhouse at Plymouth, and with fine old Colonel Coolidge and his chores and his antique grandeur. They haven't any of them the slightest intention of living in such a farmhouse if they can escape from it, or of doing the chores if they can buy a machine to do them, or of holding themselves aloof like Colonel Coolidge. But they are delighted that the President comes of such stock, and they even feel, I think, that they are stern, ascetic, and devoted to plain living because they vote for a man who is. The Coolidges are really virtuous people in the old American sense, and they have provided this generation, which is not virtuous in that sense, with an immense opportunity for vicarious virtue.

Thus we have attained a Puritanism de luxe in which it is possible to praise the classic virtues while continuing to enjoy all the modern conveniences.

May, 1926.

THE CAUSES OF POLITICAL INDIFFER-ENCE TO-DAY

I

As one contemplates the activities of politicians it seems likely that, if only there were voters somewhere who wanted it, Republican and Democratic principles could be accommodated locally to polygamy, foot binding, or voodooism. The rule is simply this: anything which helps you to carry your state is an immortal principle sanctioned by Abraham Lincoln and Thomas Jefferson.

It is not surprising, then, that national partisan politics should have come to mean so little to the ordinary voter. There are no parties, there are no leaders, there are no issues. There are parties only in the states, there are leaders only of sections, there are issues, but they are either evaded by national public men or carefully confined to the localities. There is nobody in American public life to-day who, like Roosevelt or Wilson, is really a leader in all parts of the country. Mr. Coolidge has enjoyed popularity and confidence for two years, but the record of his leadership of Congress shows that he is essentially the representative of the Eastern tariff-protected interests. Neither Western agriculture nor the Eastern exporting interests have ever laid much hold on his mind. Mr. Lowden, undoubtedly the most powerful figure in the background of Republican politics, is devoting himself wholly to that agricultural interest which Mr. Coolidge has ignored. Senator Borah has touched almost every question and has come to grips with none; with all his great promise and immense personal opportunity he has failed to transform an attractive provincial insurgency into any sort of coherent national policy. There is no need to dwell upon Messrs. Dawes, Watson, or Johnson. On the Democratic side there is Governor Smith, idol of the urban Democrats of the Northeast, but as yet wholly unknown, untried, and unexpressed on national questions. There is Governor Ritchie in Maryland, who may fairly claim to have a set of Democratic national principles, but who has not as yet a Democratic national following. And there is Senator Reed of Missouri, who has at least got this far nationally: he has made himself a holy terror to Republicans and Democrats alike.

II

The effect of these political disharmonies is to bewilder the electorate and to make the voters feel that politics is an elaborate game which has no serious and immediate consequences. This bewilderment manifests itself as complacency or as cynicism. Since 1920 the country has witnessed brazen and expensive corruption. In the amount of money involved the corruption is without parallel in our history. In its sordidness it is surely as bad and probably a little worse than the scandals of the Grant administration. This generation has known nothing so disgraceful as the carryings-on of Fall, Daugherty, and Forbes, nor anything like the Smith primary in Illinois and the Pepper-Vare primary in Pennsylvania. Fall has just been brought to trial; Daugherty was brought to trial only three or four months ago because of the exceptional energy of United States Attorney Buckner; the primary scandals were never rebuked by the leader of the Republican Party. In their public speech public men have been as complacent as possible about it all, and privately they have been prepared to explain that "Well—oh, well, you know, politics is a dirty game." Maybe it is. But only a few years ago the country was still naïve enough, was still sentimental enough, to have become violently indignant over a Cabinet officer accused of bribery. Indignation of this sort we have not known during these last few years. That, too, perhaps helps to explain why the interest in politics is at such low ebb, and why voting is not looked upon as such a very high duty. The impression has gone out from the White House that there is no use caring too much whether public officials are honest or whether elections are bought.

This persistent dampening down of popular interest in popular government has been the calculated policy of Mr. Coolidge ever since he became President. The reason given for it is that nothing must be done to distract business. The other reason for it, not given, but perfectly well understood, is that it is good politics when you are in power to discourage all manifestations of discontent. Mr. Coolidge is not exactly an ardent spirit. He is contented with little things; he is hardly suited to large thoughts and large deeds. He has not attempted them. On the contrary he has devoted himself to encouraging the people to turn their eyes away from the government. In peaceful, prosperous times not much encouragement is needed. Public spirit is at best a fragile thing when it comes into competition with the urgent demands of our private lives for money, for power, and for pleasure. So it has not been difficult for Mr. Coolidge to persuade the country that it need not take a vivid interest in public affairs.

III

Yet neither the personality of Mr. Coolidge nor

the very special political strategy which he adopted will by itself account for the lethargy of spirit which has prevailed during his administration. Under different circumstances the virtues of Mr. Coolidge would almost certainly have been looked upon as vices. Mr. Coolidge has been praised for failing to lead Congress, for failing to lead his party, for refusing to become indignant at abuses, for not having a positive policy and a constructive program. He would not have received this praise had the country not been in the mood for a negative administration.

It is the fashion to explain this mood by saying that after all the tall talk heard under Roosevelt and Wilson the country was exhausted emotionally and needed a rest. It had had its fill of idealism, of prophecy, of adventure, and of public action. It needed to forget Washington and the White House and the President, and tend to its private affairs. There is something in this explanation, of course, as there is also in the theory that the war brought a deep disenchantment with politicians, policies, and with what used to be called "progressivism." But all these explanations are obviously incomplete. For when you have said that men were tired of public affairs you have still to explain why, being tired of public affairs, they are able to indulge themselves by neglecting public affairs.

With this question we come, I think, nearer to the root of the matter. The American people, since the industrial recovery of 1922, have enjoyed an amazing prosperity. Except here and there in a few spots there has been such a surplus of wealth that practically the whole people have raised their standard of life. It was obvious that the opportunities to make money were so ample that it was a waste of time to think about politics. Nothing a man could hope to gain by voting for politicians, and by agitating for laws, was likely to be half so profitable as what he could make by participating in the boom.

The interested motives which are the driving force of political agitation were diverted to direct profit making. Now progressivism, as we have known it in the past, has arisen out of the belief of the debtors, the employees, the consumers, the farmers, that they could by changing the laws obtain a larger share of the national income. With the stupendous surplus available these last years, it has seemed to most men quicker and easier to go out and make money than to work through the cumbersome, indirect processes of political action. Thus there has been no political discontent, except in a few farming states where the new surplus of wealth was not available, and where in consequence the old progressive motives and traditions survived. The common people looked to Roosevelt and to Wilson (before 1914) for relief from poverty and economic servitude. They did not look to Mr. Coolidge for relief because they were finding it by themselves. I am not attempting to say, of course, how real or how permanent is this relief; the fact which counts is that from about 1922 on almost everybody has had the feeling that he had a lot of money in his pocket, and would soon have more. It was this feeling which robbed progressive idealism of its urgency, and made it appear abstract and unimportant.

Together with this diffused prosperity, I should set down as a fundamental cause of political indifference the rise of what may be called the New Capitalism. There is no doubt that the large corporations are now under the control of a very different kind of man than they were when Roosevelt and Bryan and LaFollette were on the warpath. The new executive has learned a great deal that his predecessor would have thought was tommyrot. His attitude toward labor, toward the public, toward his customers and his stockholders, is different. His behavior is different. His manner is different. His press agents are different. I am far from thinking he is perfect even now, but I am certain that he is vastly more enlightened and that he will take ever so much more trouble to please. He is no doubt as powerful as he ever was, but his bearing is less autocratic. He does not arouse the old antagonism, the old bitter-end fury, the old feeling that he has to be clubbed into a sense of public responsibility. He will listen to an argument where formerly he was deaf to an agitation.

Whatever may be the intrinsic good and evil of such things as the wide distribution of securities, however questionable may be some of the practices to which Professor Ripley has called attention, the net result of the new attitude on the part of capital has been to create a new attitude on the part of the public. The press agents of the corporations have been told to woo the public, and their wooing has been successful. Suspicion has died down. Yet here again we must recognize that it would not have died down if capitalism as we know it were not making most people feel quite comfortably well off.

During the last four years the actual prosperity of the people, combined with the greater enlightenment of the industrial leaders, has removed from politics all serious economic causes of agitation. There has been no pressing reason for an alignment of 'haves' and of 'have nots,' and no reader of history needs to be told that when you remove economic discontent you remove what is certainly the greatest cause, if it is not the mainspring, of political activity. Politics carried on for justice, for liberty, for prestige, is never more than the affair of a minority. For the great majority of men political ideals are almost always based upon and inspired by some kind of economic necessity and ambition.

These circumstances account for the striking differences between European and American politics. The European finance ministers have had to struggle with deficits, ours with a surplus; they have had to impose taxes, ours to reduce taxes. The European nations have had to borrow, we to lend; they to devise means of payment, we to find ways of receiving payments. They have had to struggle to raise a low standard of living, and we to protect a high standard. They have had to reconstruct and restore; we have had only to perfect and expand. To Europeans, therefore, the American situation has seemed almost idyllic, and there has appeared a great literature in Europe which discusses the American economic system, often with admiration, sometimes with envy, always with the implication that it is one of the most extraordinary phenomena in history. Here in the United States during the last few years capitalism has worked in a way which confounds those who, like most educated Europeans, were brought up to think of it according to the socialistic formula, as an industrial system destined soon to be superseded by some kind of collectivism. Events have taken a wholly unexpected turn in the United States, and the advanced thinker here and abroad suddenly finds that he is no longer advanced. His descriptions, his analyses, his programs — all assume a different course of evolution. The more or less unconscious and unplanned activities of business men are for once more novel, more daring, and in a sense more revolutionary, than the theories of the progressives. Action has moved faster than thought in these last few years, and practice is ahead of the programs.

This lag in the development of theory has had

a curious effect on political discussion. Public speakers, if they are conservative, will usually be found defending practices that their supposed clients are rapidly abandoning; if they are progressive, they will be found rather wearily and half-heartedly repeating the charges and the idealisms that were current a decade ago. The real industrial development of the day, with its momentous social consequences, hardly figures at all in public discussion. The philosophy of it is not yet understood; we have not yet learned how to talk about it. The good and the evil it contains have not yet been registered and assayed. And as a result most public controversy seems not so much like hot air as stale air. Without knowing just why, most of us feel, I think, that the current conservatism and progressivism are irrelevant. They do not satisfy our minds or grip our emotions.

IV

The questions which really engage the emotions of the masses of the people are of a quite different order. They manifest themselves in the controversies over prohibition, the Ku Klux Klan, Romanism, fundamentalism, immigration. These, rather than the tariff, taxation, credit, and corporate control, are the issues which divide the American people. These are the issues they care about. They are just beneath the surface of political discussion. In theory they are not supposed to be issues. The party platforms and the official pronouncements deal with them obliquely, if at all. But they are the issues men talk about privately, and they are the issues about which people have deep personal feelings.

These questions are diverse, but they all arise out of the same general circumstances. They arise out of the great migration of the last fifty years, out of the growth of cities, and out of the spread of that rationalism and of the deepening of that breach with tradition which invariably accompany the development of a metropolitan civilization. Prohibition, the Ku Klux Klan, fundamentalism, and xenophobia are an extreme but authentic expression of the politics, the social outlook, and the religion of the older American village civilization making its last stand against what looks to it like an alien invasion. The alien invasion is in fact the new America produced by the growth and the prosperity of America.

The evil which the old-fashioned preachers ascribe to the Pope, to Babylon, to atheists, and to the devil, is simply the new urban civilization, with its irresistible economic and scientific and mass power. The Pope, the devil, jazz, the bootleggers, are a mythology which expresses symbolically the impact of a vast and dreaded social change. The change is real enough. The language in which it is discussed is preposterous only as all mythology is preposterous if you accept it literally. The mythology of the Ku Klux Klan is a kind of primitive science, an animistic and dramatized projection of the fears of a large section of our people who have yet to accommodate themselves to the strange new social order which has arisen among them.

This new social order is dominated by metropolitan cities of which New York is the largest and most highly developed. Therefore New York has become the symbol of all that is most wicked and of all that is most alluring in modern America. But New York to-day is only what Chicago, St. Louis, Detroit, Cleveland, Jacksonville, and Miami expect to be to-morrow. It is the seat of a vast population, mixed in its origins, uncertain of its social status, rather vague about the moral code. In these metropolitan centers the ancient social bonds are loosened. The patriarchal family, the well-established social hierarchy, the old roots of belief, and the grooves of custom are all obscured by new human relationships based on a certain kind of personal independence, on individual experiment and adventure, which are yet somehow deeply controlled by fads and fashions and great mass movements.

The campaign in certain localities to forbid the teaching of "Darwinism" is an attempt to stem the tide of the metropolitan spirit, to erect a spiritual tariff against an alien rationalism which threatens to dissolve the mores of the village civilization. To many of us the effort seems quixotic, as indeed it is, judged by the intellectual standards of metropolitan life. But if we look at the matter objectively, disregarding the petty mannerisms of the movement, there is a pathos about it which always adheres to the last struggle of an authentic type of human living. The anti-evolutionists are usually less charming than Don Quixote. Perhaps that is because they have not been transfigured by an artist. They are at any rate fighting for the memory of a civilization which in its own heyday, and by its own criteria, was as valid as any other.

The anti-evolution bills are, of course, a comparatively trivial symptom of this profound maladjustment. The overt struggle turns politically on two questions: on the Eighteenth Amendment and on the nomination of Governor Alfred E. Smith. The struggle over these two issues implicates all the antagonisms between the older America and the new. The Eighteenth Amendment is a piece of legislation embodied in the Constitution which attempts to impose the moral ideals of the villages upon the whole nation. The force behind the Eighteenth Amendment is the Anti-Saloon League, which is the political arm of the evangelical churches in the small communities. The financial and political strength of the Anti-Saloon League is derived from the members of these churches, chiefly Methodist and Baptist, with other denominations divided but following these militant sects. And the strength of these sects in the last analysis arises from the spiritual isolation of communities which have not yet been radically invaded by the metropolitan spirit. The defense of the Eighteenth Amendment has, therefore, become much more than a mere question of regulating the liquor traffic. It involves a test of strength between social orders, and when that test is concluded, and if, as seems probable, the Amendment breaks down, the fall will bring down with it the dominion of the older civilization. The Eighteenth Amendment is the rock on which the evangelical church militant is founded, and with it are involved a whole way of life and an ancient tradition. The overcoming of the Eighteenth Amendment would mean the emergence of the cities as the dominant force in America, dominant politically and socially as they are already dominant economically.

V

The alignment of the new cities against the older villages traverses the nominal political alignment of the two great parties. In New York State, for example, the Republican Party as a state organization is divided and broken. There is much more community of thought and feeling between Republicans and Democrats in New York City, in Buffalo, Rochester, Syracuse, and Albany, than there is between the urban and the rural Republicans. The unity of the Republican Party in New York is like the unity of the Democrats in the nation: a unity of politicians interested in offices supplemented by the prestige of a name and a tradition. There is no unity of interest, of principle, or of program.

A similar condition exists in almost every state where there are powerful cities—in Massachusetts for Boston, in Pennsylvania for Pittsburgh and Philadelphia, in Ohio for Cleveland and Cincinnati, in Illinois for Chicago, in New Jersey for that urban conglomeration known as Hudson County, in Missouri for St. Louis. Both parties are cracking under the strain. Both maintain the appearance of unity by political deals and the compromise of principles. The well-known fact that parties have become meaningless is due to this internal division. They dare not take definite positions for fear of alienating one or the other of their irreconcilable factions.

For reasons which are not altogether clear the conflict has first become overt in the Democratic Party. The convention of 1924 was the scene of the first great, though inconclusive, phase of the struggle. All the signs indicate that the next phase, in 1928, will be at least as sharp and perhaps more decisive. In 1924 the urban democracy rallied around Governor Smith of New York, the village democracy around Mr. McAdoo. The urban Democrats in 1924 controlled a little more than one third of that convention. Since 1924 they have gained in strength and by 1928 they should control at least half of the convention. This change of their position from a minority to a majority faction is not due to the personality or to the leadership of Governor Smith. It is due to a growth of self-consciousness which is developing the latent strength of the city electorates. They are beginning to feel their oats. They are throwing off their sense of inferiority. They are beginning to demand the recognition which is due their intrinsic importance.

The outcome of the struggle within the Democratic Party is, of course, obscure. One can be certain of nothing except that the rapid growth of the cities at the expense of the countryside is bound at last to result in the political domination of the cities. This may come soon. It may be somewhat delayed. It will come. The first great result may be the disunion of the Democratic Party and perhaps even the rupture of the Solid South. If that is the result the ascendancy of the Republicans may be temporarily confirmed, but it will be followed almost certainly by a realignment of Republicans as well as of Democrats.

For the two parties live by taking in each other's washing. The unity of the one is dependent upon the unity of the other. The grip of the Eastern industrial Republicans on the national organization rests at last on the fact that in the South there is a Republican machine but no Republican electorate. If ever the South should break away from the Democrats, a Republican Party would appear in the South. The appearance of a Republican Party in the South would make the South as unmanageable to the Republicans of the Northeast as the Republican Party of the West now is.

These prospects are not alluring to men whose

lives are bound up with the existing party system. They promise nothing but trouble for them personally. They call for an effort of thought which is distressing, and they open up issues for which political leaders, trained between 1890 and 1910, are not prepared. It is not surprising, then, that our political leaders are greatly occupied in dampening down interest, in obscuring issues, and in attempting to distract attention from the realities of American life.

February, 1927.

THE CATHOLICISM OF AL SMITH

I

FOR more than a century most Americans have believed both that a religion was no test of a man's fitness for public office and that only a Protestant should be elected President of the United States. This paradox has often been noticed, but until about the year 1923 it was a merely theoretical difficulty without practical importance. For until after the second election of Governor Smith there had never been a serious contender for the Presidency who was not a Protestant.

Since the rise of Smith, desperate efforts have been made by Democratic politicians to find some way of avoiding a direct test of the question whether a Catholic is eligible to be President. They have pointed out that he is a wet, that he belongs to Tammany Hall, that he is a cockney. But these objections however sincere and weighty have been regarded by the mass of people as unreal. Protestants and Catholics alike have felt in their bones that any Democrat who can be elected Governor of New York four times would under ordinary circumstances have an irresistible attraction for the politicians. They may cross their hearts and say that they have no objection to Governor Smith's Catholicism, and they may even think they mean it, and yet they will not be believed.   Governor Smith is so clearly available by every conventional test, except that of his religion, that the conviction has now become set, among the newer Americans of the cities, and is now, I think, irremovable that his Catholicism alone stands in the way of his nomination.   They may misunderstand the deeper sources of the opposition to Smith as an incarnation of the city, but their misunderstanding is nevertheless a fact of dominating importance.

Since the Catholic voters are a predominant part of the Democratic Party outside of the South, the question of Smith's nomination has become one of life and death to the party.   He cannot be rejected without alienating an absolutely essential part of the votes on which the only possible chance of a Democratic victory depends.   There are now some twenty million Catholics in the United States.   They are no longer, as they were a generation ago, largely confined to a class who do the menial work and do not have to be taken into account in the government of the country.   They are a substantial and powerful part of the electorate, and few of them are in a mood to acquiesce under a concrete test in the unwritten law that they are second-class citizens who cannot aspire, no matter what their other qualifications, to the highest office in the land.

These are the circumstances, roughly, which have
made Mr. Marshall's open letter in the *Atlantic
Monthly,* and Governor Smith's reply, an event of
such historic importance. Mr. Marshall on his
side formulated in the shape of a documented argument the inarticulate fear which inspires the old
American tradition against allowing a Catholic to
become President. In effect he summarized what
remains in the modern world of the medieval claim
of the Church to temporal power. The Governor on
his side made a declaration of belief as an American
Catholic which amounts to a complete disavowal of
the medieval theory of the Church's power. In this
disavowal he claimed to speak for American Catholics, and prelates qualified to speak for the American
hierarchy have publicly approved his utterances. The
net result of the correspondence, therefore, has been
to make articulate, definite, and formal the separa-
tion, in questions of polity, between the mass of
American Catholics and the historic claims of the
Roman Church. There are precedents in the history
of American Catholicism for the position which the
Governor has taken. But never has the distinction
between Catholicism in twentieth century America
and the Catholicism of the Middle Ages been stated
with such unqualified clearness.

II

The momentous character of Governor Smith's
declaration can be understood only by realizing

exactly what was the question Mr. Marshall put to him and exactly what was his answer.   Mr. Marshall's argument can be compressed into very simple form.   The Roman Catholic Church teaches in the words of Pope Leo XIII that "the Almighty has appointed the charge of the human race between two powers, the ecclesiastical and the civil, the one being set over divine, the other over human things." But who, asks Mr. Marshall, shall decide what are the divine and what the human things?   He then cites Pope Pius IX who said "to say in the case of conflicting laws enacted by Two Powers (*i.e.* civil and ecclesiastical), the civil law prevails, is error." Against this he cites the decision of the Supreme Court (Watson vs. Jones) that religious liberty in America is qualified because religious "practices inconsistent with the peace and safety of the State shall not be justified."   And from this he argues that since the Roman Church claims the right to decide what things are within its jurisdiction, whereas the American theory makes the civil power the judge of its own jurisdiction, no faithful Catholic can give unreserved allegiance to the civil power in America.

The argument comes down then to this crucial point: suppose the Church claimed that a question affecting education or marriage or foreign affairs was to be determined by the principles of the Roman Church, and suppose the executive, legislature, and courts of the United States claimed that the question was to be determined by them, which authority, the ecclesiastical or the civil, would Governor Smith or any other good Catholic recognize as final?

Governor Smith's reply, which avowedly was made after consultation with priests of his Church, is as follows:

". . . In the wildest dreams of your imagination you cannot conjure up a possible conflict between religious principle and political duty in the United States, except on the unthinkable hypothesis that some law were to be passed which violated the common morality of all God-fearing men.   If you conjure up such a conflict how would a Protestant resolve it?   Obviously by the dictates of his conscience.   That is exactly what a Catholic would do. There is no ecclesiastical tribunal which would have the slightest claim upon the obedience of Catholic communicants in the resolution of such a conflict."

Governor Smith's answer to the fundamental question as to which jurisdiction he would recognize as final is that he would follow the dictates of his own conscience in each particular case.   This is a very far-reaching declaration.   It amounts to saying that there is an authority higher than the utterances of the Church or the law of the land, namely "the common morality of all God-fearing men," and that the conscience of Alfred E. Smith, and of every other individual, is the final interpreter of whether that common morality has been violated.

If Governor Smith were not a Catholic in good standing, if the reply had not been made with the approval of members in good standing of the Catholic hierarchy, one would be tempted to say that he has avowed the essential Protestant doctrine of the right of private judgment in all matters where any secular interest was involved.   But said by him, under these extraordinary circumstances, buttressed with citations from American Catholic prelates, there is only one possible conclusion which can be reached: it is that for American Catholics there is absolutely no distinction between their attitude and the attitude of Protestants.   The ultimate authority, says Governor Smith, is conscience.   He makes no qualifications.   He does not say conscience as authoritatively guided by the Pope; on the contrary, he says, quite explicitly, that the guidance of the Pope is to be judged, wherever a secular interest is affected, by the determinations of conscience.   Citing Archbishop Ireland on "the Church's attitude toward the State," he affirms that "both Americanism and Catholicism bow to the sway of personal conscience."

If any form of words could put an end to so ancient and deep-seated a controversy as that between Protestantism and Catholicism, this avowal would do it.   For the deep Protestant fear that Catholics submit their consciences to an alien power with its seat in Rome is here answered by the radical assertion that for American Catholics their consciences are a higher authority than their Catholicism. I call it a radical assertion, for there is little doubt that Governor Smith in adopting Archbishop Ireland's statement has aligned himself unqualifiedly with that wing of his Church which is furthest removed from the medieval ideal of a truly catholic and wholly authoritative synthesis of all human interests. Governor Smith is the latest, and by no means the least, of a long line of Catholics who have wholly forgotten, indeed may never even have heard of, what the Church conceived itself to be in the days of its greatest worldly splendor and ambitions. Certainly one detects in him no lingering trace of the idea, speculatively at least so magnificent even to those who, like this writer, were not reared in the Catholic tradition—the idea of Catholicism not as a religious sect but as a civilization. The Catholicism of Governor Smith is the typical modern post-reformation nationalistic religious loyalty in which the Church occupies a distinct and closely compartmented section of an otherwise secular life.

The position of American Catholics like Governor Smith is very close to being what J. N. Figgis calls "the final stage in that transposition of the spheres of Church and State which is, roughly speaking, the net result of the Reformation." For "in the Middle Ages the Church was not a State, it was the State; the State or rather the civil authority [for a separate society was not recognized] was merely the police department of the Church. The latter took over from the Roman Empire its theory of the absolute and universal jurisdiction of the supreme authority, and developed it into the doctrine of the *plenitudo potestatis* of the Pope, who was the supreme dispenser of law, the fountain of honor, including regal honor, and the sole legitimate earthly source of power . . . the supreme 'judge and divider' among nations, the guardian of international right, the avenger of Christian blood. All these functions have passed elsewhere, and the theory of omnipotence, which the Popes held on the plea that any action might come under their cognizance so far as it concerned morality, has now been assumed by the State on the analogous theory that any action, religious or otherwise, so far as it becomes a matter of money, or contract, must be matter for the courts."

I said that the position occupied by Governor Smith came very close to being that of this "final stage" in modern development where the omnipotence of the State is substituted for the medieval omnipotence of the Church. It is not quite clear just what is Mr. Marshall's position, although it seems to me to imply that "Americanism" means the absolute supremacy of the civil power in all matters which the civil power chooses to consider as within its jurisdiction. If this is what Mr. Marshall really thinks, it is not what Governor Smith thinks. For the Governor puts his personal conscience above the secular claims both of Church and State, and denies the absolute jurisdiction of both.

This, I venture to believe, is not only a sounder

Americanism in the historic meaning of that term,
but a more truly enlightened and civilized doctrine
than that which is now so widely preached to justify
the idolatry of the political state. For it is all
very well to argue that the Church of Rome shall
not have the last word in deciding what things men
shall render unto Caesar, and what to God. But it
would be a sinister philosophy indeed which went on
to say that Caesar must have the last word as to
what things belong to Caesar, and what to God. This
is just as real a dilemma, in many ways it is a more
practical dilemma, than any with which Mr. Marshall confronts Catholics. Does Mr. Marshall claim
that the political state must be as absolute to-day as
the Church claimed to be in the Middle Ages? His
silence implies that he is not disposed to examine
the credentials of Caesar. Yet I doubt whether
after consideration Mr. Marshall would finally say
that Americanism requires that a man shall sur-
render to Caesar, acting through popular and legislative majorities, through proletarian dictatorships or
plutocracies, dominion over all the interests of life.

III

For this idolatry of the political state is merely a
barbarous Machiavellianism which afflicts the modern world and finds its ultimate logical expression
in communism and in fascism. The founders of
the American Republic had seen all they cared to see
of the absolute civil power. When they founded a
government they conceived its powers as limited and

derived, and they would have been horrified at the notion, now so common that it is apparently a commonplace to Mr. Marshall, that the United States Government had a jurisdiction so absolute that it could define the extent of its jurisdiction.

Governor Smith in pointing out that "conscience" is superior both to Catholicism and Americanism is closer to the spirit of the founders of the Republic than Mr. Marshall who assumes, at least by implication, that Americanism must mean the superiority of Americanism to any religious teaching, and to any conception of morals. Governor Smith is not only more truly American in the historic sense of the word, but he is more enlightened in his premises. For in denying the temporal power of the Pope, he does not fall into the very easy error of attributing universal power to the State. He leaves the question of civil obedience where it must always remain in a complicated world for any man who is neither a fanatic nor a theorist; to adjustment in specific cases by the conscience of the individual acting upon the evidence before it. And by leaving it there he puts upon the civil power and the ecclesiastical alike the burden, which ought always to be theirs, of justifying themselves continually in practice to whatever wisdom there may be in the consciences of men.

May, 1927.

BRYAN AND THE DOGMA OF MAJORITY RULE

DURING the Dayton trial there was much discussion about what had happened to Mr. Bryan. How had a progressive democrat become so illiberal? How did it happen that the leader of the hosts of progress in 1896 was the leader of the hosts of darkness in 1925?

It was said that he had grown old. It was said that he was running for President. It was said that he had the ambition to lead an uprising of fundamentalists and prohibitionists. It was said that he was a beaten orator who had found his last applauding audience in the backwoods. And it was said that he had undergone a passionate religious conversion.

No matter whether the comment was charitable or malicious, it was always an explanation. There

was always the assumption that Mr. Bryan had
changed, and that, in changing, he had departed from
the cardinal tenets of his political faith. Mr. Bryan
vehemently denied this and, on reflection, I am now
inclined to think he was right. We were too hasty.
Mr. Bryan's career was more logical and of a piece
than it looked. There was no such contradiction,
as most of us assumed, in the spectacle of the Great
Commoner fighting for the legal suppression of
scientific teaching.

He argued that a majority of the voters in Tennessee had the right to decide what should be taught
in their schools. He had always argued that a
majority had the right to decide. He had insisted on
their right to decide on war and peace, on their right
to regulate morals, on their right to make and
unmake laws and lawmakers and executives and
judges. He had fought to extend the suffrage so
that the largest possible majority might help to
decide; he had fought for the direct election of senators, for the initiative and referendum and direct
primary, and for every other device which would
permit the people to rule. He had always insisted
that the people should rule. And he had never
qualified this faith by saying what they should rule
and how. It was no great transformation of
thought, and certainly it was not for him an aban-
donment of principle to say that, if a majority in
Tennessee was fundamentalist, then the public

schools in Tennessee should be conducted on fundamentalist principles.

To question this right of the majority would have seemed to him as heretical as to question the fundamentalist creed. Mr. Bryan was as true to his political as he was to his religious faith. He had always believed in the sanctity of the text of the Bible. He had always believed that a majority of the people should rule. Here in Tennessee was a majority which believed in the sanctity of the text. To lead this majority was the logical climax of his career, and he died fighting for a cause in which the two great dogmas of his life were both at stake.

Given his two premises, I do not see how it is possible to escape his conclusions. If every word of the first chapter of Genesis is directly inspired by an omniscient and omnipotent God, then there is no honest way of accepting what scientists teach about the origin of man. And if the doctrine of majority rule is based on the eternal and inherent rights of man, then it is the only true basis of government, and there can be no fair objections to the moral basis of a law made by a fundamentalist majority in Tennessee. It is no answer to Mr. Bryan to say that the law is absurd, obscurantist, and reactionary. It follows from his premises, and it can be attacked radically only by attacking his premises.

This first premise—that the text of the Bible was written, as John Donne put it, by the Secretaries of the Holy Ghost—I shall not attempt to discuss here. There exists a vast literature of criticism. I am interested in his second premise: that the majority is of right sovereign in all things. And here the position is quite different. There is a literature of dissent and of satire and denunciation. But there exists no carefully worked-out higher criticism of a dogma which, in theory at least, constitutes the fundamental principle of nearly every government in the Western World. On the contrary, the main effort of political thinkers during the last few generations has been devoted to vindicating the rights of masses of men against the vested rights of clerics and kings and nobles and men of property. There has been a running counter attack from those who distrusted the people, or had some interest in opposing their enfranchisement, but I do not know of any serious attempt to reach a clear understanding of where and when the majority principle applies.

Mr. Bryan applied it absolutely at Dayton, and thereby did a service to democratic thinking. For he reduced to absurdity a dogma which had been held carelessly but almost universally, and thus demonstrated that it was time to reconsider the premises of the democratic faith. Those who believed in democracy have always assumed that the majority should rule. They have assumed that, even if the majority is not wise, it is on the road to wisdom, and that with sufficient education the people would learn how to rule. But in Tennessee the people used their power to prevent their own children from learning, not merely the doctrine of evolution, but the spirit and method by which learning is possible. They had used their right to rule in order to weaken the agency which they had set up in order that they might learn how to rule. They had founded popular government on the faith in popular education, and they had used the prerogatives of democracy to destroy the hopes of democracy.

After this demonstration in Tennessee it was no longer possible to doubt that the dogma of majority rule contains within it some sort of deep and destructive confusion.

II

In exploring this dogma it will be best to begin at the very beginning with the primitive intuition from which the whole democratic view of life is derived. It is a feeling of ultimate equality and fellowship with all other creatures.

There is no worldly sense in this feeling, for it is reasoned from the heart: "there you are, sir, and there is your neighbor. You are better born than he, you are richer, you are stronger, you are handsomer, nay, you are better, wiser, kinder, more likable; you have given more to your fellow men and taken less than he. By any and every test of intelligence, of virtue, of usefulness, you are demonstrably a better man than he, and yet—absurd as it sounds—these differences do not matter, for the last part of him is untouchable and incomparable and unique and universal." Either you feel this or you do not; when you do not feel it, the superiorities that the world acknowledges seem like mountainous waves at sea; when you do feel it they are slight and impermanent ripples upon a vast ocean. Men were possessed by this feeling long before they had imagined the possibility of democratic government. They spoke of it in many ways, but the essential quality of feeling is the same from Buddha to St. Francis to Whitman.

There is no way of proving the doctrine that all souls are precious in the eyes of God, or, as Dean Inge recently put it, that "the personality of every man and woman is sacred and inviolable." The doctrine proceeds from a mystical intuition. There is felt to be a spiritual reality behind and independent of the visible character and behavior of a man. We have no scientific evidence that this reality exists, and in the nature of things we can have none. But we know, each of us, in a way too certain for doubting, that, after all the weighing and comparing and judging of us is done, there is something left over which is the heart of the matter. Hence our conviction when we ourselves are judged that mercy is more just than justice. When we know the facts as we can know only the facts about ourselves, there is something too coarse in all the concepts of the intelligence and something too rough in all the standards of morality. The judgments of men fall upon behavior. They may be necessary judgments, but we do not believe they are final. There is something else, which is inadmissible, perhaps, as evidence in this world, which would weigh mightily before divine justice. Each of us knows that of himself, and some attribute the same reserved value to others. Some natures with a genius for sympathy extend it to every one they know and can imagine; others can barely project it to their wives and children. But even though few really have this sympathy with all men, there is enough of it abroad, reënforced perhaps with each man's dread of his fate in the unknown, to establish the doctrine rather generally. So we execute the murderer, but out of respect for an inviolable part of him we allow him the consolation of a priest and we bury him respectfully when he is dead. For we believe that, however terrible was his conduct, there is in him, nevertheless, though no human mind can detect it, a final quality which makes him part of our own destiny in the universe.

I can think of no inherent reason why men should entertain this mystical respect for other men. But it is easy to show how much that we find best in the world would be lost if the sense of equality and fellowship were lost. If we judged and were judged by our visible behavior alone, the inner defenses of civility and friendship and enduring love would be breached. Outward conduct is not good enough to endure a cold and steady analysis. Only an animal affection becomes habitual and reflected in mystical respect can blind people sufficiently to our faults. They would not like us enough to pardon us if all they had to go on was a strict behaviorist account of our conduct. They must reach deeper, blindly and confidently, to something which they know is likable although they do not know why. Otherwise the inequalities of men would be intolerable. The strong, the clever, the beautiful, the competent, and the good would make life miserable for their neighbors. They would be unbearable with their superiorities, and they would find unbearable the sense of inferiority they implanted in others. There would be no term upon the arrogance of the successful and the envy of the defeated. For without the mystic sense of equality the obvious inequalities would seem unalterable.

These temporal differences are seen in perspective by the doctrine that in the light of eternity there are no differences at all.

III

It is not possible for most of us, however, to consider anything very clearly or steadily in the light of eternity. The doctrine of ultimate human equality cannot be tested in human experience; it rests on a faith which transcends experience. That is why those who understood the doctrine have always been ascetic; they ignored or renounced worldly goods and worldly standards. These things belonged to

Caesar. The mystical democrat did not say that they should not belong to Caesar; he said that they would be of no use to Caesar ultimately, and that, therefore, they were not to be taken seriously now.

But in the reception of this subtle argument the essential reservation was soon obscured. The mystics were preaching equality only to those men who had renounced their carnal appetites; they were welcomed as preachers of equality in this world. Thus the doctrine that I am as good as you in eternity, because all the standards of goodness are finite and temporary, was converted into the doctrine that I am as good as you are in this world by this world's standards. The mystics had attained a sense of equality by transcending and renouncing all the standards with which we measure inequality. The populace retained its appetites and its standards and then sought to deny the inequalities which they produced and revealed.

The mystical democrat had said, "gold and precious stones are of no account"; the literal democrat understood him to say that everybody ought to have gold and precious stones. The mystical democrat had said, "beauty is only skin deep"; and the literal democrat preened himself and said, "I always suspected I was as handsome as you." Reason, intelligence, learning, wisdom, dealt for the mystic only with passing events in a temporal world and could help men little to fathom the ultimate meaning of creation; to the literal democrat this incapacity of reason was evidence that one man's notion was intrinsically as good as another's.

Thus the primitive intuition of democracy became the animus of a philosophy which denied that there could be an order of values among men. Any opinion, any taste, any action was intrinsically as good as any other. Each stands on its own bottom and guarantees itself. If I feel strongly about it, it is right; there is no other test. It is right not only as against your opinion, but against my own opinions, about which I no longer feel so strongly. There is no arbitrament by which the relative value of opinions is determined. They are all free, they are all equal, all have the same rights and powers.

Since no value can be placed upon an opinion, there is no way in this philosophy of deciding between opinions except to count them. Thus the mystical sense of equality was translated to mean in practice that two minds are better than one mind and two souls better than one soul. Your true mystic would be horrified at the notion that you can add up souls and that the greater number is superior to the lesser. To him souls are imponderable and incommensurable; that is the only sense in which they are truly equal. And yet in the name of that sense of equality which he attains by denying that the worth of a soul can be measured, the worldly democrats have made the mere counting of souls

the final arbiter of all worth.   It is a curious misunderstanding; Mr. Bryan brought it into high relief
during the Tennessee case.   The spiritual doctrine
that all men will stand at last equal before the throne
of God meant to him that all men are equally good
biologists before the ballot box of Tennessee.   That
kind of democracy is quite evidently a gross material-
ization of an idea that in essence cannot be
materialized.   It is a confusing interchange of two
worlds that are not interchangeable.

IV

Although the principle of majority rule derives a
certain sanctity from the mystical sense of equality,
it is really quite unrelated to it.   There is nothing in
the teachings of Jesus or St. Francis which justifies
us in thinking that the opinions of fifty-one percent
of a group are better than the opinions of forty-nine
percent.   The mystical doctrine of equality ignores
the standards of the world and recognizes each soul
as unique; the principle of majority rule is a device
for establishing standards of action in this world by
the crude and obvious device of adding up voters.
Yet owing to a confusion between the two, the
mystical doctrine has been brutalized and made
absurd, and the principle of majority rule has
acquired an unction that protects it from criticism.
A mere political expedient, worth using only when it
is necessary or demonstrably useful to the conduct

of affairs, has been hallowed by an altogether adventitious sanctity due to an association of ideas with a religious hope of salvation.

Once we succeed in disentangling this confusion of ideas, it becomes apparent that the principle of majority rule is wholly alien to what the humane mystic feels. The rule of the majority is the rule of force. For while nobody can seriously maintain that the greatest number must have the greatest wisdom or the greatest virtue, there is no denying that under modern social conditions they are likely to have the most power. I say likely to have, for we are reminded by the recent history of Russia and of Italy that organized and armed minorities can under certain circumstances disfranchise the majority. Nevertheless, it is a good working premise that in the long run the greater force resides in the greater number, and what we call a democratic society might be defined for certain purposes as one in which the majority is always prepared to put down a revolutionary minority.

The apologists of democracy have done their best to dissemble the true nature of majority rule. They have argued that by some mysterious process the opinion to which a majority subscribes is true and righteous. They have even attempted to endow the sovereign majority with the inspiration of an infallible church and of kings by the grace of God. It was a natural mistake. Although they saw clearly enough that the utterances of the church were the decisions of the ruling clergy, and that the divine guidance of the king was exercised by his courtiers, they were not prepared to admit that the new sovereign was a purely temporal ruler. They felt certain they must ascribe to the majority of the voters the same supernatural excellence which had always adhered to the traditional rulers. Throughout the nineteenth century, therefore, the people were flattered and mystified by hearing that deep within a fixed percentage of them there lay the same divine inspiration and the same gifts of revelation which men had attributed previously to the established authorities.

And then just as in the past men had invented a mythical ancestry for their king, tracing his line back to David or Æneas or Zeus himself, so the minnesingers of democracy have invented their own account of the rise of popular government. The classic legend is to be found in the theory of the Social Contract, and few naïve democrats are without traces of belief in this legend. They imagine that somehow "the people" got together and established nations and governments and institutions. Yet the historic record plainly shows that the progress of democracy has consisted in an increasing participation of an increasing number of people in the management of institutions they neither created nor willed. And the record shows, too, that new numbers were allowed to participate when they were powerful enough to force their way in; they were

enfranchised not because "society" sought the bene-
fits of their wisdom, and not because "society"
wished them to have power; they were enfranchised
because they had power, and giving them the vote
was the least disturbing way of letting them exercise
their power. For the principle of majority rule is
the mildest form in which the force of numbers can
be exercised. It is a pacific substitute for civil war
in which the opposing armies are counted and the
victory is awarded to the larger before any blood is
shed.

Except in the sacred tests of democracy and in
the incantations of the orators, we hardly take the
trouble to pretend that the rule of the majority is
not at bottom a rule of force. What other virtue
can there be in fifty-one percent except the brute fact
that fifty-one is more than forty-nine? The rule of
fifty-one percent is a convenience; it is for certain
matters a satisfactory political device, it is for others
the lesser of two evils, and for still others it is
acceptable because we do not know any less troublesome method of obtaining a political decision. But
it may easily become an absurd tyranny if we regard
it worshipfully, as though it were more than a political device. We have lost all sense of its true meaning when we imagine that the opinion of fifty-one
percent is in some high fashion the true opinion of
the whole hundred percent, or indulge in the
sophistry that the rule of a majority is based upon
the ultimate equality of man.

V

At Dayton Mr. Bryan contended that in schools supported by the state the majority of the voters had a right to determine what should be taught. If my analysis is correct, there is no fact from which that right can be derived except the fact that the majority is stronger than the minority. It cannot be argued that the majority in Tennessee represented the whole people of Tennessee; nor that fifty-one Tennesseeans are better than forty-nine Tennesseeans; nor that they were better biologists, or better Christians, or better parents, or better Americans. It cannot be said they are necessarily more in tune with the ultimate judgments of God. All that can be said for them is that there are more of them, and that in a world ruled by force it may be necessary to defer to the force they exercise.

When the majority exercises that force to destroy the public schools, the minority may have to yield for a time to this force, but there is no reason why they should accept the result. For the votes of a majority have no intrinsic bearing on the conduct of a school. They are external facts to be taken into consideration like the weather or the hazard of fire. Guidance for a school can come ultimately only from educators, and the question of what shall be taught as biology can be determined only by biologists. The votes of a majority do not settle anything here and they are entitled to no respect whatever. They may

be right or they may be wrong; there is nothing in
the majority principle which will make them either
right or wrong. In the conduct of schools, and especially as to the details of the curriculum, the majority
principle is an obvious irrelevance. It is not even a
convenient device as it is in the determination say of
who shall pay the taxes.

VI

But what good is it to deny the competence of the
majority when you have admitted that it has the
power to enforce its decisions? I enter this denial
myself because I prefer clarity to confusion, and the
ascription of wisdom to fifty-one percent seems to
me a pernicious confusion. But I do it also because
I have some hope that the exorcising of the super-
stition which has become attached to majority rule
will weaken its hold upon the popular imagination,
and tend therefore to keep it within convenient
limits. Mr. Bryan would not have won the logical
victory he won at Dayton if educated people had not
been caught in a tangle of ideas which made it seem
as if the acknowledgment of the absolutism of the
majority was necessary to faith in the final value of
the human soul. It seems to me that a rigorous
untangling of this confusion might help to arm the
minority for a more effective resistance in the future.

March, 1926.

H. L. MENCKEN

A review of his "Notes on Democracy"

HERE in two hundred pages is Mr. Mencken's philosophy. Here are the premises of that gargantuan attack upon the habits of the American nation which has made Mr. Mencken the most powerful personal influence on this whole generation of educated people. I say personal influence, for one thing this book makes clear, and that is that the man is bigger than his ideas.

If you subtract from this book the personality of H. L. Mencken, if you attempt to restate his ideas in simple, unexcited prose, there remains only a collection of trite and somewhat confused ideas. To discuss it as one might discuss the ideas of first-rate thinkers like Russell, Dewey, Whitehead, or Santayana would be to destroy the book and to miss its importance. Though it purports to be the outline of a social philosophy, it is really the highly rhetorical expression of a mood which has often in the past and may again in the future be translated into thought. In the best sense of the word the book is sub-rational: it is addressed to those vital preferences which lie deeper than coherent thinking.

The most important political books are often of this sort. Rousseau's *Social Contract* and Tom Paine's *Rights of Man* were far inferior as works of the mind to the best thought of the eighteenth century, but they exerted an incalculably great influence because they altered men's prejudices. Mr. Mencken's book is of the same sort. The democratic phase which began in the eighteenth century has about run its course. Its assumptions no longer explain the facts of the modern world and its ideals are no longer congenial to modern men. There is now taking place a radical change of attitude not merely toward parliamentary government but toward the whole conception of popular sovereignty and majority rule. This change is as radical in its way as that which took place, say between 1776 and 1848.

In the United States Mr. Mencken's is the most powerful voice announcing the change. The effect of his tremendous polemic is to destroy, by rendering it ridiculous and unfashionable, the democratic tradition of the American pioneers. This attack on the divine right of demos is an almost exact equivalent of the earlier attacks on the kings, the nobles, and the priests. He strikes at the sovereign power, which in America to-day consists of the evangelical churches in the small communities, the proletarian masses in the cities, and the organized smaller business men everywhere. The Baptist and Methodist sects, the city mobs, and the Chamber of Commerce are in power. They are the villains of the piece. Mr. Mencken does not argue with them. He lays violent hands upon them in the conviction, probably correct, that you accomplish results quicker by making your opponent's back teeth rattle than by laboriously addressing his reason. Mr. Mencken, moreover, being an old newspaper man, has rather strong notions about the capacity of mankind to reason. He knows that the established scheme is not supported by reason but by prejudice, prestige, and reverence, and that a good joke is more devastating than a sound argument. He is an eminently practical journalist, and so he devotes himself to dogmatic and explosive vituperation. The effect is a massacre of sacred cows, a holocaust of idols, and the poor boobs are no longer on their knees.

Mr. Mencken is so effective just because his appeal is not from mind to mind but from viscera to viscera. If you analyze his arguments you destroy their effect. You cannot take them in detail and examine their implications. You have to judge him totally, roughly, approximately, without definition, as you would a barrage of artillery, for the general destruction rather than for the accuracy of the individual shots. He presents an experience, and if he gets you, he gets you not by reasoned conviction, but by a conversion which you may or may not be able to dress up later as a philosophy. If he succeeds with you, he implants in you a sense of sin, and then he revives you with grace, and disposes you to a new and somewhat fierce pride in a non-gregarious excellence.

One example will show what happens if you pause to analyze his ideas. The thesis of this whole book is that we must cease to be governed by "the inferior four-fifths of mankind." Here surely is a concept which a thinker would have paused to define. Mr. Mencken never does define it, and, what is more, he quite evidently has no clear idea of what he means. Sometimes he seems to think that the difference between the inferior four-fifths and the superior one-fifth is the difference between the "haves" and the "have nots." At other times he seems to think it is the difference between the swells and the nobodies, between the well born and those who come "out of the gutter." At other times he abandons these worldly distinctions and talks and thinks about "free spirits," a spiritual élite, who have no relation either to income or to a family tree. This vagueness as to whether the superior one-fifth are the Prussian Junkers or the Pittsburgh millionaires, or the people who can appreciate Bach and Beethoven, persists throughout the book.

This confusion is due, I think, to the fact that he is an outraged sentimentalist. Fate and his own curiosity have made him a connoisseur of human ignorance. Most educated men are so preoccupied with what they conceive to be the best thought in the field of their interest, that they ignore the follies of uneducated men. A Jacques Loeb would spend very little of his time on biology as taught in an Oklahoma high school. Even William James, who was more interested in the common man than any great philosopher of our time, was looking always for grains of wisdom in the heaps of folly. But Mr. Mencken is overwhelmingly preoccupied with popular culture. He collects examples of it. He goes into a rage about it. He cares so much about it that he cannot detach himself from it. And he measures it not by relative standards, but by the standards which most educated men reserve for a culture of the first order. He succeeds, of course, in establishing a *reductio ad absurdum* of the shibboleths of liberals. That is worth doing. But it is well to know what you are doing, and when Mr. Mencken measures the culture of the mass by the cultural standards of the élite, he is not throwing any real light on the modern problem. He is merely smashing a delusion by means of an effective rhetorical device.

I doubt, however, if he is aware that he is using a rhetorical device. When he measures the popular culture by the standards of the élite, the humor is all on the surface. The undertone is earnest and intensely sincere. One feels that Mr. Mencken is deeply outraged because he does not live in a world where all men love truth and excellence and honor.

I feel it because I detect in this book many signs of
yearning for the good old days. When Mr.
Mencken refers to feudalism, to kings, to the Prussian aristocracy, to any ordered society of the ancient
régime, he adopts a different tone of voice. I don't
mean to say that he talks like an *émigré* or like a
writer for the *Action Française,* but it is evident to
me that his revolt against modern democratic society
exhausts his realism, and that the historic alternatives are touched for him with a romantic glamour.
The older aristocratic societies exist only in his
imagination; they are idealized sufficiently to inhibit
that drastic plainness of perception which he applies
to the democratic society all about him.

The chief weakness of the book, as a book of
ideas, arises out of this naïve contrast in Mr.
Mencken's mind between the sordid reality he knows
and the splendid society he imagines. He never
seems to have grasped the truth that the thing he
hates is the direct result of the thing he most admires.
This modern democracy meddling in great affairs
could not be what it is but for that freedom of
thought which Mr. Mencken, to his everlasting
credit, cares more about than about anything else. It
is freedom of speech and freedom of thought which
have made all questions popular questions. What
sense is there then in shouting on one page for a
party of "liberty," and on another bewailing the
hideous consequences? The old aristocracies which
Mr. Mencken admires did not delude themselves

with any nonsense about liberty. They reserved
what liberty there was for a privileged élite, knowing
perfectly well that if you granted liberty to every
one you would have sooner or later everything that
Mr. Mencken deplores. But he seems to think that
you can have a privileged, ordered, aristocratic
society with complete liberty of speech. That is as
thoroughgoing a piece of utopian sentimentalism as
anything could be. You might as well proclaim yourself a Roman Catholic and then ask that excerpts
from *The American Mercury* and the works of
Charles Darwin be read from the altar on the first
Sunday of each month. If Mr. Mencken really
wishes an aristocracy he will have to give up liberty
as he understands it; and if he wishes liberty he will
have to resign himself to hearing *homo boobiens*
speak his mind.

What Mr. Mencken desires is in substance the
distinction, the sense of honor, the chivalry, and
the competence of an ideal aristocracy combined
with the liberty of an ideal democracy. This is an
excellent wish, but like most attempts to make the
best of both worlds, it results in an evasion of the
problem. The main difficulty in democratic society
arises out of the increasing practice of liberty. The
destruction of authority, of moral values, of cultural
standards is the result of using the liberty which
has been won during the last three or four centuries.
Mr. Mencken is foremost among those who cry for
more liberty, and who use that liberty to destroy

what is left of the older tradition. I do not quarrel
with him for that. But I am amazed that he does
not see how fundamentally the spiritual disorder he
fights against is the effect of that régime of liberty
he fights for. Because he fails to see that, I think
he claims too much when he says that he is engaged
in a diagnosis of the democratic disease. He has
merely described with great emphasis the awful pain
it gives him.

In the net result these confusions of thought are
a small matter. It is no crime not to be a philosopher. What Mr. Mencken has created is a personal
force in American life which has an extraordinarily
cleansing and vitalizing effect. How else can you
explain the paradox of his popularity, and the cer-
tainty that before he dies he will find himself, like
Bernard Shaw to-day, one of the grand old men,
one of the beloved patriarchs of his time? How in
this land where all politicians, pedagogues, peasants,
etc., etc., are preposterous, has Henry L. Mencken,
not yet aged fifty, become the pope of popes? The
answer is that he has the gift of life. His humor
is so full of animal well-being that he acts upon his
public like an elixir. The wounds he inflicts heal
quickly. His blows have the clean brutality of a
natural phenomenon. They are directed by a warm
and violent but an unusually healthy mind which is
not divided, as most minds are, by envy and fear
and ambition and anxiety. When you can explain
the heightening effect of a spirited horse, of a swift

athlete, of a dancer really in control of his own body, when you can explain why watching them you feel more alive yourself, you can explain the quality of his influence.

For this reason the Mencken manner can be parodied, but the effect is ludicrous when it is imitated. The same prejudices and the same tricks of phrase employed by others are usually cheap and often nasty. I never feel that in Mr. Mencken himself even when he calls quite harmless people cockroaches and lice. I do not care greatly for phrases like that. They seem to me like spitting on the carpet to emphasize an argument. They are signs that Mr. Mencken writes too much and has occasionally to reach for the effect without working for it. I think he is sometimes lazy, and when he is lazy he is often unfair, not in the grand manner but in the small manner. And yet his wounds are clean wounds and they do not fester. I know, because I have fragments of his shellfire in my own skin. The man is admirable. He writes terribly unjust tirades, and yet I know of nobody who writes for his living who will stay up so late or get up so early to untangle an injustice. He often violates not merely good taste according to the genteel tradition, but that superior kind of good taste according to which a man refuses to hurt those who cannot defend themselves.

Nevertheless I feel certain that in so far as he has influenced the tone of public controversy he has elevated it. The Mencken attack is always a frontal attack. It is always explicit. The charge is all there. He does not leave the worst unsaid. He says it. And when you have encountered him, you do not have to wonder whether you are going to be stabbed in the back when you start to leave and are thinking of something else.

I have not written this as a eulogy, but as an explanation which to me at least answers the question why Henry L. Mencken is as popular as he is in a country in which he professes to dislike most of the population. I lay it to the subtle but none the less sure sense of those who read him that here is nothing sinister that smells of decay, but that on the contrary this holy terror from Baltimore is splendidly and exultantly and contagiously alive. He calls you a swine and an imbecile, and he increases your will to live.

December, 1926.

SINCLAIR LEWIS

I

T HE career of Mr. Lewis is usually divided into two periods: an earlier in which he wrote popular fiction without much success, and a later, beginning with "Main Street," in which he tried only to please himself and had a huge success. Roughly speaking, this second period began with the inauguration of Warren Harding. Mr. Lewis has continued to flourish under Calvin Coolidge.

This is not, I imagine, a mere coincidence. The election of 1920 marked the close of that period of democratic idealism and of optimism about the perfectibility of American society, which began in its modern phase with Bryan, was expressed for a while by Roosevelt, and culminated in the exaltation and the spiritual disaster under Wilson. By 1920 the American people were thoroughly weary of their old faith that happiness could be found by public work, and very dubious about the wisdom of the people. They had found out that the problem of living is deeper and more complex than they had been accustomed to think it was. They had, moreover, become rich. They were ready for an examination of themselves.

Mr. Lewis was in a position to supply the demand. For he too had outlived his political illusions, having passed beyond the socialist idealism of Helicon Hall. At the moment when he sat down to please himself by writing "Main Street," in the heroic mood of one who abandons the quest of money and applause, a vast multitude was waiting for him with more money and applause than he had ever dreamed about.

In this first success there was apparently no element of calculation. It so happened that the personal mood of Sinclair Lewis suited exactly the mood of a very large part of the American people. Very quickly he became a national figure. "Main Street," "Babbitt," and, in a certain measure, "Arrowsmith," became source books for the new prejudices and rubber stamps with which we of the Harding-Coolidge era examined ourselves.

II

Although we are all endowed with eyes, few of us see very well. We see what we are accustomed to see, and what we are told to see. To the rest of what is about us we are largely anesthetic, for we live in a kind of hazy dream bent on our purposes. For the apprehension of the external world, and of that larger environment which is invisible, we are almost helpless until we are supplied with patterns of seeing which enable us to fix objects clearly amidst the illegible confusion of experience. When we find a pattern which works well, in that it allows us to feel that we have made a large area of reality our own, we are grateful, and we use that pattern until it is threadbare. For to invent new patterns requires more genius than most of us have, and to deal with life freshly in all its variety is much too much trouble for preoccupied men. As a mere matter of economy in time and trouble, we demand simple and apparently universal stereotypes with which to see the world.

Mr. Lewis has an extraordinary talent for inventing stereotypes. This talent is uninhibited, for he is wholly without that radical skepticism which might make a man of equal, or even greater, genius hesitate at substituting new prejudices for old. "This is America," he says in an italicized foreword; "this Main Street is the continuation of Main Streets everywhere." Now a writer without this dogmatism of the practical man, and with a greater instinct for reality, could not have written these words. He would have remembered that the world is not so simple. But what he would have gained in truthfulness, he would have lost in influence. He would probably not have induced a large part of the nation to adopt his line of stereotypes as a practical convenience for daily use along with the telephone, the radio, the syndicated newspaper, and similar mechanical contrivances for communicating with other men.

Mr. Lewis has prospered by inventing and marketing useful devices for seeing the American scene quickly. His psychological inventions are being used by millions of Americans to perceive and express their new, disillusioned sense of America. They are wholly mechanical and they are completely standardized now that they have passed into common use. Because of Mr. Lewis's success in fixing the conception of Main Street, it is now very difficult to see any particular Main Street with an innocent eye. A Babbitt is no longer a man; he is a prejudice.

The art of creating these prejudices consists, in Mr. Lewis's case, of an ability to assemble in one picture a collection of extraordinarily neat imitations of lifelike details. Had his gift been in a different medium he could have manufactured wax flowers that would make a man with hay fever sneeze; he could have crowed so much like a rooster that the hens would palpitate. He has a photo- and phonographic memory with an irresistible gift of mimicry. But since his business is the creation of types rather than of living characters, he does not photograph and mimic individuals. Babbitt is not a man; he is assembled out of many actual Babbitts. The effect is at once lifelike and weird. As with an almost perfect scarecrow the thing is so much like life that it nearly lives. Yet it is altogether dead. It is like an anatomical model of an average man, a purely theoretical concept which has no actual existence. For in any living man the average qualities are always found in some unique combination.

But just because Mr. Lewis's creations are composed of skillful imitations of details, they are extraordinarily successful as stereotypes. The Babbitt pattern covers no actual Babbitt perfectly, but it covers so many details in so many Babbitts that it is highly serviceable for practical purposes. The veracity in detail is so striking that there is no disposition to question the verity of the whole.

III

It is not going too far to say that Mr. Lewis has imposed his conception of America on a very considerable part of the reading and writing public. To-day they see what he has selected out of the whole vast scene. Now Mr. Lewis is a reformer. He does not assemble his collection of details with the disinterested desire to hold a mirror up to nature. He wishes to destroy what he dislikes and to put something better in its place; he is rarely relieved of an overpowering compulsion to make or break something. Yet this particular zeal is no necessary part of his great talent for mimicry. For he might conceivably have loved life more than his own purposes, and have written a human comedy. Or he might have felt that sense of their destiny which makes all human creatures tragic. Or he might have been filled with a feeling for the mystery that enshrouds so temporary a thing as man, and then he would have confessed that after you have studied their behavior no matter how accurately from the outside, there is much in all human souls that remains to be known. But Mr. Lewis is not a great artist. He has a great skill. He himself is a practical man with the practical man's illusion that by bending truth to your purposes, you can make life better.

There was a moment, I think, when Mr. Lewis was tempted to use his talent with that serene disinterestedness by which alone wisdom comes. I refer to that passage in one of the early chapters of "Main Street" when for the first time Mr. Lewis describes Main Street. Until I reread the book recently I had forgotten that in this early stage Mr. Lewis presents the reader with two quite contrasting versions of the same scene. One is the version we all remember, a dull, fly-specked, timidly gaudy spectacle of human vacuity. The other version, which he soon allows the reader to forget, is romantic, exciting, and full of promise. There is no doubt that at this juncture Mr. Lewis meant to say: What you see in Main Street will depend on what you are; it all depends on who is looking at it. In order to emphasize this notion he gives you first the Main Street which Carol Kennicott sees on her first walk in Gopher Prairie, and then immediately following the identical aspects of Main Street as seen by Bea Sorenson who is just off a lonely farm.

Carol is a comparatively sophisticated person; at least she does not belong to the prairies but to a town which with "its garden-sheltered streets and aisles of elms is white and green New England reborn." Carol, moreover, came from a cultivated home with a "brown library" in which she "absorbed" Balzac and Rabelais and Thoreau and Max Mueller. It might reasonably be objected, I know, that Carol never absorbed anything, let alone such heady stuff as Rabelais. But what Mr. Lewis meant to say is plain enough. It is that Carol came from a background which predisposed her to dislike the raw ugliness of Main Street civilization. And having said that, he introduced Bea by way of contrast and justice to show how delightful Main Street would look to a peasant mind.

"It chanced that Carol Kennicott and Bea Sorenson were viewing Main Street at the same time." Carol looks through the fly-specked windows of the Minniemashie House and sees only the row of rickety chairs with the brass cuspidors; Bea is thrilled by the swell traveling man in there—probably been to Chicago lots of times. At Dyer's drug store Carol sees a greasy marble soda fountain with an electric lamp of red and green and curdled-yellow mosaic shade; to Bea the soda fountain is all lovely marble with the biggest shade you ever saw—all different kinds of colored glass stuck together.

There is a humility in this passage which might have become the seed of a much richer wisdom than his regular practice exhibits. Here for a moment Mr. Lewis used his gift without self-righteousness. Here in this interlude he was willing to show some courtesy to the souls of other people. He was willing even to admit that their feelings are authentic. In this mood, had he been able to retain it, he might have risen above the irritations of his time and his clique, have given even the devil his due, and become the creator of a great American comedy of manners instead of the mere inventor of new prejudices.

But to have done that he would have had to care more about human beings than about his own attitude toward them. Apparently that was impossible for him. He cannot for long detach himself from the notion that what Sinclair Lewis feels about Main Street, about Babbittry, about the Protestant churches is of primary importance. What he feels would have more importance if he had great insight as well as great sight, if he had fine taste instead of sharp distastes, if he had salient intuition as to what moves people as well as an astounding memory of how they look to him when they move. Then his figures might have come alive, and been something more than a synthetic mass of detail which serves as the butt for the uncritical, rebellious yearning of the author.

Had he a real interest in character, and not such a preoccupation with behavior, he would have expressed his view of the world through all his characters, and not merely through one mouthpiece. He would have given you Main Street through Dr. Kennicott and Bea and Vida and Percy Bresnahan, instead of giving you Kennicott, Bea, Vida, and Bresnahan through Carol. For that young woman staggers under the burden of the weighty message she is forced to carry. "There—she meditated—is the newest empire of the world; the Northern Middle West . . . an empire which feeds a quarter of the world—yet its work is merely begun. They are pioneers, these sweaty wayfarers, for all their telephones and bank accounts and automatic pianos and coöperative leagues. And for all its fat richness, theirs is a pioneer land. What is its future? she wondered."

She meditated! She wondered! Did she really, or did Sinclair Lewis? I ask the question in no captious spirit. This uncertainty as to who is talking and who is seeing the detail he reports pervades all of Mr. Lewis's books, and prevents him from achieving that "more conscious life" for which Carol yearns in phrases that are borrowed from H. G. Wells. When Mr. Lewis described Bea's walk on Main Street, he remembered for a moment what he usually forgets, that a more conscious life is one in

which a man is conscious not only of what he sees,
but of the prejudices with which he sees it.

IV

Though he is absorbed in his own vision of things,
Mr. Lewis is curiously unaware of himself. He is
aware only of the object out there. Carol, Babbitt,
Arrowsmith and Frank Shallard have sharp eyes
but vague spirits. Mr. Lewis is sophisticated enough
to realize how they flounder about, and he laughs at
them. But this laughter is not comic, it is protective.
It is a gesture of defense by a man who knows that
some mature reader, say Mr. Mencken, is going
to laugh, and it is better to laugh first. It is not the
carefree laughter of a man who is detached from the
rather adolescent rebellion which he is describing.
On the contrary, he is absorbed by it. Underneath
their sardonic and brutal tone, these novels are
extraordinarily earnest and striving. "Main Street,"
"Babbitt" and "Arrowsmith" are stories of an individual who is trying to reform the world, or to find
salvation by escaping it.

Carol fusses with "fanlights and Galsworthy"
brightly painted furniture, and a separate bedroom.
She runs away to Washington but returns to Gopher
Prairie, saying: "I may not have fought the good
fight but I have kept the faith." Babbitt on his
sleeping porch dreams of the fairy child, frets with
"veiled rebellions," escapes to the Maine woods,

thinks he has been "converted to serenity," isn't,
returns to Zenith, and, like Carol, at the end makes
a speech: "Tell 'em to go to the devil." Martin
Arrowsmith also takes to the woods, escaping from
his wife's blue and gold velvet limousine, and at the
end says: "We'll plug along for two or three years,
and maybe we'll get something permanent—and
probably we'll fail."

Dr. Arrowsmith is the only one who may have
found what he wanted. He has fled from the
barbarians and their gauds, he has left "a soft
bed for a shanty bunk in order to be pure. For he
had perceived the horror of the shrieking, bawdy
thing called Success."

"I am sorry," says Gottlieb when he has to tell
Arrowsmith that his great discovery belongs to some
one else. "I am sorry you are not to have the fun
of being pretentious and successful—for a while.
. . . Martin, it is nice that you will corroborate
D'Herelle. This is science: to work and not to care
—too much—if somebody else gets the credit."

Arrowsmith is saved by embracing the religion of
science. But for Carol and for Babbitt and for
Shallard there is no religion available which they
can embrace, and therefore, there is no salvation.
Mr. Lewis knew what to do with Arrowsmith. For
there is an ideal in science to which a modern man
can give himself and find peace. But there is no
ideal for Carol or Babbitt. They would not be
helped by "believing in" science, no matter how

devoutly.   Only Arrowsmith who can do scientific
work can be saved by it.   Only Arrowsmith finds a
god to love whom no man can possess and no man
can cajole.

This is the point of Mr. Lewis's greatest insight
into the human predicament.   There is an unconscious pathos about it, for obviously the religion
which Arrowsmith embraces, ascetic, disinterested,
purified, is for Mr. Lewis like some fine mystery seen
at a distance.   That there might be a path of salvation like it for his ordinary characters, though in
other ways, is too difficult for him to believe.   It
would be hard for me to believe.   But it would have
been possible to put the rebellion of Carol and the
yearning of Babbitt in the perspective of an understanding of how, as Spinoza says, all things excellent
are as difficult as they are rare.   They might have
failed, but their failure would have been measured
against a spiritual insight as fine as Arrowsmith's.
Then at least the author would have understood the
failure of his characters to understand themselves.

That degree of insight Mr. Lewis does not attain.
He can report what he sees; having known about
the religion of science, he was able to report it in
Arrowsmith.   But in Carol and in Babbitt he was
projecting only his own spirit, and when he attempts
to make it articulate, he becomes literary and fum-
bling: "It was mystery which Carol had most
lacked in Gopher Prairie . . . where there were
no secret gates opening upon moors over which one

might walk by moss-deadened paths to strange, high adventures in an ancient garden." Babbitt escapes from Zenith only when he is asleep, when he is drunk, and vicariously when his son tells the family to go to the devil. For Carol and Babbitt are worldlings, and for the worldling there is no personal salvation. He must either conquer the world and remake it, though in that he will almost surely fail, or he must escape into his dreams.

V

The America of Mr. Lewis is dominated by the prosperous descendants of the Puritan pioneers. He has fixed them at a moment when they have lost the civilized traditions their ancestors brought from Europe, and are groping to find new ways of life. Carol is the daughter of a New Englander who went west taking with him an English culture. In Carol that culture is little more than a dim memory of a more fastidious society; it merely confuses her when she tries to live by it in Gopher Prairie. Babbitt is the descendant of a pioneer; he is completely stripped of all association with an ordered and civilized life. He has no manners, no coherent code of morals, no religion, no piety, no patriotism, no knowledge of truth and no love of beauty. He is almost completely decivilized, if by civilization you mean an understanding of what is good, better and best in the satisfaction of desire, and a knowledge of the customs, the arts, and the objects which can give these satisfactions.

Carol and Babbitt inherit the culture of the pioneers who were preoccupied with the business of establishing themselves in a new world. But for them there is no wilderness to subdue, there are no Indians to fight, they have houses and sanitation and incomes. They have the leisure to be troubled; for they really have very little to do. They have nothing to do which exhausts them sufficiently to distract them when they ask themselves: What is it all about? Is is worth while? Their ancestors came as emigrants, and they divested themselves for the voyage of that burden of ancient customs which, with all its oppressions, made life a rite, and gave it shape and significance. For Carol and Babbitt this European heritage has been liquidated until all that remains of it is a series of prohibitions called morality, and a habit of church attendance without a god they adore or an ideal of holiness with which they can commune. Their religion has become a creed which they do not understand; it has ceased to be, as it was in Catholic Europe, or even in theocratic New England, a way of life, a channel of their hopes, an order with meaning. They are creatures of the passing moment who are vaguely unhappy in a boring and senseless existence that is without dignity, without grace, without purpose. They are driven by they know not what compulsions, they are ungoverned and yet unfree, the sap of life does not reach them, their taproots having been cut. In that great transplantation of peoples which has made America, not many have as yet struck down deep into the nourishing earth. And those who have not are only dimly alive, like Carol, like Babbitt, who are weedy and struggling to bloom.

The "splendid indefinite freedoms" for which Carol yearns are an emancipation from the frayed remnants of the heritage her Yankee forefathers brought with them to America. That stern culture nerved the pioneers to hardship. It merely makes Carol nervous. She will, however, soon be free of this bondage. In the big city, where her creator has preceded her, she will be bothered no longer. She will be a free metropolitan spirit, like Mr. Lewis, free to do anything, free to disbelieve, free to scorn her past, free to be free.

VI

The prophet of this metropolitan spirit, toward which Carol reaches out, is Mr. Mencken. Now Mr. Mencken is a true metropolitan. Mr. Lewis is a half-baked metropolitan. He has just arrived in the big city. He has the new sophistication of one who is bursting to write to the folks back home and let them know what tremendous fellows we are who live in the great capitals. There is more than a touch of the ex-naif in Mr. Lewis, not a little of the snobbery of the newly arrived. For he has as yet none of the radical skepticism of the true metropolitan. His iconoclasm is merely a way of being cocksure that the household gods of Gopher Prairie are a joke. There is no evidence in his writing that he knows or cares much about the good things which the world city contains, as Mr. Mencken does with his German music, his fine sense of learning, and his taste for speculation about genus homo apart from his manifestations on Main Street. Mr. Lewis is proud to belong to the great city, he enjoys the freedom from the Main Street tabus. But he is as restless in the big city as he is in Gopher Prairie. Unlike Mr. Mencken who is quite comfortable, happy, and well settled, as he shells the outer barbarians from his fastness at Baltimore, Mr. Lewis is forever running about the world and giving out interviews about how Main Street is to be found everywhere. He is probably right for he takes it with him wherever he goes.

The terrible judgments which he pronounces upon the provincial civilization of America flow from the bitterness of a revolted provincial. Mr. Mencken is savage at times, but there is a disinfectant on his battle-ax, because he is in no way turned morbidly in upon himself. Mr. Mencken is not a revolted Puritan. He is a happy mixture of German gemuethlichkeit and Maryland cavalier. But Mr. Lewis is still so enmeshed with the thing he is fighting that he can never quite strike at it gallantly and with a light heart. He is too much a part of the revolt he describes ever for long to understand it. That, it seems to me, is why he cannot distinguish between a sample of human ignorance and the deep-seated evil which is part of this world. Everything is in the foreground and in the same focus, ugly furniture and hypocrisy, dull talk and greed, silly mannerisms and treachery. This makes his books so monotonously clever. He will take the trouble to be as minutely devastating about poor Babbitt's fondness for a trick cigarette lighter as about the villainies of Elmer Gantry. He puts everything in the same perspective, because he has no perspective. Like Carol, he is annoyed by almost everything he sees in the provinces, and all his annoyances are about equally unpleasant to him.

For he is still in that phase of rebellion where the struggle to get free is all-absorbing. Of the struggle that comes after, of the infinitely subtler and more bewildering problems of mature men, he has written nothing, and not, I think, thought much. It cannot be an accident that in his whole picture gallery there is not the portrait of one wholly mature personality, of one man or woman who has either found his way in the new world, or knows clearly why he has not. There are such personalities in America, and Mr. Lewis is not a writer who tells less than he knows, or would fail to draw such a character if he had ever actually realized his existence. But Mr. Lewis's characters are all adolescent, and they express an adolescent rebellion.

VII

Mr. Lewis's revolt against the Puritan civilization had of course to include an attack on the evangelical churches. "That small pasty-white Baptist Church had been the center of all his emotions, aside from hell-raising, hunger, sleepiness, and love. . . . He had, in fact, got everything from the Church and Sunday School, except, perhaps any longing whatever for decency and kindness and reason." This is Mr. Lewis's conclusion at the beginning of "Elmer Gantry," and the rest of the book is a sockdologer to prove it.

Had Mr. Lewis followed the pattern of the earlier novels he would have taken as his theme the struggle of an increasingly liberal clergyman to square his real faith with his creed. He would have made a clerical Arrowsmith. There is, in fact, such a character in the book, Frank Shallard, who symbolizes the central confusion of the churches. But Mr. Lewis merely sketches him in, and then lynches him with the help of the Ku Klux Klan. He was not greatly interested in Shallard. His hatred of the Protestant churches was too hot for any patient and sympathetic interest in the men who are somewhat vaguely trying to make organized religion suit the needs and doubts of modern men. He is not conscious as yet that somewhere in the ferment of religious discussion, Carol and Babbitt will have to find an equivalent for the salvation which Arrowsmith achieves. All that, which is after all the main question, Mr. Lewis ignores completely. For his central character he has chosen an absolute villain. And so "Elmer Gantry," instead of being the story of a fundamentalist like Babbitt beset by doubts, or of a liberal like Carol, who has more impulse than direction, the book is a synthesis of all the villainies, short of murder, which the most villainous villain could commit.

Elmer Gantry is not, however, the portrait of a villain as such. It is the study of a fundamentalist clergyman in the United States, portrayed as utterly evil in order to injure the fundamentalists. The calumny is elaborate and deliberate. Mr. Lewis hates fundamentalists, and in his hatred he describes them as villains. This was, I believe, a most intolerant thing to do. It is intellectually of a piece with the sort of propaganda which says that John Smith is an atheist, and that he beats his wife; that Jones is a radical, and that he cheats at cards; that Robinson is a free trader, and that he robs the till.

Mr. Lewis is a maker of stereotypes. He had successfully fixed his versions of Main Street and of' Babbittry on the American mind. Then, quite unscrupulously, it seems to me, he set out to stereotype the fundamentalist as an Elmer Gantry. His method was his old device of assembling details, but in his choice of details he was interested only in those which were utterly damning. It is as if he had gone to the clipping files of an atheist society, pored over the considerable collection of reports about preachers "arrested for selling fake stock, for seducing fourteen-year-old girls in orphanages under their care, for arson, for murder" (p. 378) and out of this material had then concocted the portrait of a clergyman. This is a stock method of the propagandist, and one of the least admirable. There is no truth in it. There is no human dignity in it. It is utterly irrational. If it succeeds it merely creates new prejudices for old, and if it fails it leaves a nasty smell behind it.

I have seen "Elmer Gantry" described as the greatest blow ever struck in America at religious hypocrisy. It may be a great blow. It may, for all I know, be another "Uncle Tom's Cabin." But it is none the less a foul blow, and I do not think the cause of "decency, kindness and reason," which Mr. Lewis espouses on page 28, is greatly helped by adapting toward fundamentalists the essential spirit of the Ku Klux Klan. The practice of describing your opponent as a criminal ought to be reserved for low disordered minds with white sheets over their heads. A novelist who pretends to be writing in behalf of a civilized life ought not himself to behave like a barbarian.

The animating spirit of "Elmer Gantry" is the bigotry of the anti-religious, a bigotry which is clever but as blind as any other. Were it not that the discussion of religion seems always to stir up exceptional passions, the quality of this book might well alarm Mr. Lewis's friends. For until he wrote it, he had his hatred under control. "Main Street" is a rather sentimental book at bottom. "Babbitt" is pervaded by an almost serene kindliness. "Arrowsmith" reaches moments of spiritual understanding. But "Elmer Gantry" is written with a compulsion to malice as if the author could hardly hold himself. The industriousness of his hatred is extraordinary. He gives himself to an abandoned fury which is fascinating as a mere spectacle of sustained ferocity. You say to yourself: What endurance! What voluptuous delight this fellow takes in beating and kicking this effigy, and then beating him and kicking him again! If only he keeps it up, the sawdust in Gantry will be spilled all over the ground!

For in "Elmer Gantry" the revolted Puritan has become fanatical. The book is a witch-burning to make an atheist holiday.

VIII

There has been some curiosity as to what Mr. Lewis would tackle next. Bets have been laid, I hear, on the politician, the editor, the lawyer, the professor, the business executive. It is a fairly important question because Mr. Lewis is a very important man. But what interests me is whether Mr. Lewis will reach maturity, or remain arrested in his adolescent rebellion. After "Arrowsmith" one would have said that he was beginning to be free of

that shapeless irritation and yearning which Carol
Kennicott typifies.   But after "Elmer Gantry" one
cannot be so sure.   The hatreds are turned inward,
as if the effort to escape had failed and become
morbid.   There is some sort of crisis in this aston-
ishing career, which is not yet resolved.

June, 1927.

THE NATURE OF THE BATTLE OVER
CENSORSHIP

I

NOT long ago I was at work in my study writing, when, as was her custom, the lady across the way burst into song. There was something about that lady's voice which prevented the use of a human intelligence, and I called upon the janitor to give her my compliments and then silence her. She replied with a good deal of conviction that this was a free country and she would sing when the spirit moved her; if I did not like it, I could retire to the great open spaces.

The lady and I both love liberty, I think. But she loves her liberty whereas I love mine. There does not seem to be a theory of liberty which can be used to decide between us. Lord Acton, for example, was a great historian of the problem of liberty, but as between the lady and myself, I see no help from him when he says that "by liberty I mean the assurance that every man shall be protected in doing what he believes his duty against the influence of authority and majorities, custom and opinion." It was the lady's custom to feel it her duty to practice her singing at the precise moment when I felt it my duty to write an article. The janitor never seemed so completely convinced as I was that mine was much the higher form of duty until he had had a chance on the day after Christmas to compare the lady's gift with mine. Then apparently he read John Stuart Mill, learned that "the sole end for which mankind are warranted, individuals or collectively, in interfering with the liberty of action of any of their number, is self-protection." I got protection and it cost me a box of Corona Coronas, twenty-five dollars, and an old overcoat.

I am somewhat persuaded that no one has ever succeeded in defining the area of liberty more precisely than I did in this case. The classic attempts by Milton and Mill end, if you examine them, in vagueness and compromise. Milton, for example, would have granted freedom of opinion to every one but the Papists and the Atheists; Mill was prepared to suppress any one who did "evil" to "others," leaving it to the others, it would seem, to decide what was evil. Had Milton been asked why Papists and Atheists should be denied the freedom he asked for Dissenters, he would probably have said that they would abuse their freedom. Mill argued that if you gave too much liberty to some men there would be none left for other men. He may have been right, but when you admit this to be true you have disposed of the claim that there is a clear and universal doctrine of liberty.

A theory of liberty is usually stated in general terms, but in fact its real meaning in concrete cases is derived from the nature of these cases themselves. Milton worked out his doctrine of liberty as a weapon which the Puritans could use against the Stuarts; Mill wrote for Victorian England during the ascendancy of the middle class, in that short interval between the downfall of the squirearchy and before the rise of the great corporations. He addressed himself to a section of the English people which did not then contemplate the possibility of really serious divisions of opinion.

The history of Luther's ideas shows how closely related is a theory of liberty to the specific needs of the man who preaches it. When Luther first came into conflict with the Holy See he stood very much alone. There was at that time no Protestant Church, the German princes had not taken him up, he had not worked out a Protestant theology. At this juncture he made his famous utterance on behalf of liberty, saying that "Princes are not to be obeyed when they command submission to superstitious errors, but their aid is not to be invoked in support of the word of God." Facing a bull of excommunication, living in fear of assassination, he preached that heretics must be converted by Scripture and not by fire, otherwise the hangman would be the greatest doctor. But later when the religious revolution had won in Germany, it developed, like all revolutions, beyond anything that Luther had desired. In the name of that right of private judgment and dissent which he had proclaimed against Leo X, there arose heresies within the heresy, the sects of Zwingli and the Anabaptists, and the red jacobinism of the Peasants' War. Luther was horrified at these threats against the security of the Church he had founded. "Out of the gospel and divine truth come devilish lies," he cried, "from the blood in our body comes corruption." The devil, he said, having failed to put him down by the help of the Pope, was seeking his destruction through the preachers of treason and blood. He exhorted the nobles to crush the rebels without mercy. "If there are innocent persons among them, God will surely save and preserve them as He did with Lot and Jeremiah."

Lord Acton, from whom I have taken this account, says that in appealing to the sword Luther had in reality reverted to his original teaching, and that the notion of liberty, whether civil or religious, was hateful to his despotic nature and contrary to his interpretation of Scripture. It remains a fact that Luther had at one time preached the revolutionary doctrine of the right of private judgment, and that this doctrine was worked out to justify his own rebellion against Rome.

II

Heywood Broun and Margaret Leech say in their book on Anthony Comstock that "anything remotely bearing upon sex was to his mind obscene." This helps to explain Comstock, but it is quite misleading if it is meant as an account of Comstockery. This crusading is not a one-man affair, and the psychopathology of the vice crusader does not, I think, give a convincing explanation of his success in enlisting the support of the community. Obviously American society from the Civil War to the World War was not composed entirely or even largely of Anthony Comstocks. Yet for forty years the vice crusade was carried on with the consent of the community punctuated only here and there by the jeers of a minority. Comstock got his support not because of what he believed about the uncleanness of sex but because of what he did toward suppressing those particular manifestations of sex which respectable people wished to have suppressed.

The patrons of his society, the public officials, the clergy, and the fathers and mothers who backed him were not much interested in, and many were no doubt embarrassed by, his idiotic assaults on September Morn and the nude classics. They were thinking of the tons of plainly indecent books and pictures he destroyed rather than the occasional masterpiece which he insulted.

A realistic study of censorship will show, I believe, that it is almost wholly directed against the unadjusted outsiders. It is not the idea as such which the censor attacks, whether it be heresy or radicalism or obscenity. He attacks the circulation of the idea among the classes which in his judgment are not to be trusted with the idea.

The censor himself may be cited as proof of this assertion that the danger is believed to be not in the idea itself but in the peculiar corruptibility of a certain part of the community. The censor exposes himself daily to every corrupting influence. I do not know, of course, what goes on in the dreams of those who compile the Index Expurgatorius, spend their days reading bolshevik pamphlets in the Department of Justice, see all the prohibited films and read all the dirty books. They may in their unconscious minds come to doubt God, insult the flag, and despise chastity. But whatever the private consequences may be, outwardly the censors remain doubly convinced of the sanctity of the institution they are protecting. No one has ever been known to decline to serve on a committee to investigate radicals on the ground that so much exposure to their doctrines would weaken his patriotism, nor on a vice commission on the ground that it would impair his morals. Anything may happen inside the censor, but what counts is that in his outward appearances after his ordeal by temptation he is more than ever a paragon of the conforming virtues. Perhaps his appetites are satisfied by an inverted indulgence, but to a clear-sighted conservative that does not really matter. The conservative is not interested in innocent thoughts. He is interested in loyal behavior.

Apart from certain residual tabus which have the power to cause irrational fear, the essence of censorship has always been, not to suppress subversive ideas as such, but to withhold them from those who are young or unprivileged or otherwise undependable. The purpose of censorship is to prevent overt rebellion against the state, the church, the family, and the economic system. Where there is no danger of overt action there is rarely any interference with freedom.

That is why there has so often been amazing freedom of opinion within an aristocratic class which at the same time sanctioned the ruthless suppression of heterodox opinion among the common people. When the Inquisition was operating most effectively against the bourgeois who had lapsed into heresy, the princes of the Church and the nobles enjoyed the freedom of the Renaissance. There are indeed historians who point out that the Inquisition was not concerned with Jews, Mohammedans and infidels but almost entirely with Christians who had lapsed. For the evil which the Inquisition attacked was not disbelief as such but disloyalty to the Church.

An old Roman maxim said: *de internis non iudicat praetor*, the judge is not concerned with subjective things. Neither is the censor. He does not bother about the internal freedom of an aristocracy, the free speculation which has long been practiced within the Jesuit order, the private candor of politicians and journalists, the unimpressed realism of bankers about business men. Opinions in such a medium are free because they are safe. There is no organic disposition to run wild because the mind is free.

For purposes of argument the advocates of censorship will often pretend that they are worried about the intrinsic viciousness of an idea. Advocates of censorship are often muddle-headed and therefore not clear as to why they are doing what they are doing. But actions speak louder than words, and when you look at censorship as a whole it is plain that it is actually applied in proportion to the vividness, the directness, and the intelligibility of the medium which circulates the subversive idea. The moving picture is perhaps the most popular medium of expression there is; it speaks clearly to the lowest and the most immature intelligence. It is therefore forbidden to present many scenes which the theater is free to present. There are less theaters and the seats cost more. In America, at least, the theater is now largely confined to the metropolitan centers, and it is patronized by a well-to-do, comparatively mature, and sophisticated audience. It is only when a play goes into a long run and begins to be seen by the very general public, as was "The Captive," for example, that the authorities are compelled to pay much attention to protests from the guardians of morality. The scandal about "The Captive" was at bottom its success. Had it been played for a limited run in a theater attended by the sophisticated, it would not have been clubbed to death. But when "The Captive" had run four months on Broadway it had exhausted its mature audience; it was then being patronized by much simpler people, and it was from them and from those who heard from them that the demand for suppression arose and gradually became irresistible.

The newspapers and magazines of general circulation are much freer than the stage. They discuss regularly matters which if presented on the stage would bring out the police reserves. Men are much less moved by what they read than by what they see, and literacy is a recent and uncertain accomplishment of the human race. The proprietors of the tabloids found this out a few years ago and it has been a very profitable discovery. They have produced a new type of paper which is consciously adapted to a low and hurried intelligence. But the essence of tabloid journalism is that it caters with extreme skill to the unadjusted and unprivileged part of the community. It offers them not rebellion but vicarious satisfaction, and therefore it is a kind of narcotic bolshevism as distinguished from the stimulant bolshevism that Lenin preached. There is some protest against the tabloids, but it is not as yet very severe, because the tabloids are in effect a substitute for rebellion rather than a cause of it. Nevertheless they are suspect because, like the moving picture, they reach the suspect classes, and one may confidently predict that if censorship is ever applied to American newspapers it will be due to some breach of the peace which is ascribed to the tabloids. Unless they turn respectable, as some of them show signs of doing, the logic of their formula will compel them to explore newer and newer excitements. They will experiment until at last they bring down upon themselves the wrath of the established community.

The novel is even freer than the press to-day because it is an even denser medium of expression. And in the jargon of a learned treatise a man may if he likes discuss with equanimity the advantages and disadvantages of incest among the Egyptian Pharaohs, or assassination as a method of social reform. For the practical limitations on the freedom of thought and speech are fixed by the estimate of those who have the power to suppress as to how effectively a dangerous idea is being presented to those who might be disposed to rebel.

III

Any one who with a moderately objective mind examines our own great controversies about freedom and suppression cannot fail, I think, to realize how little their avowed theory has to do with the attitude men take. The arguments which men used to justify the nullification of the Fifteenth Amendment in Georgia are now heard in Massachusetts to justify the nullification of the Eighteenth Amendment. The same corporate interests which object to regulation at home as an intolerable form of paternalism insist when they go abroad that the government shall protect them as if they were helpless children. The word "liberty" as used to-day may mean the open shop if an employer is speaking, a closed shop if a labor leader is speaking. There is no commonly accepted definition of liberty. The government of human affairs consists in finding a compromise among conflicting interests: liberty is the watchword used by an interest to justify it in doing what it would like to do, and authority is the watchword of an interest that does not wish to be interfered with by some other interest while it is doing what it wishes to do.

In concrete questions the verbal encounter throws little light on the issue. Suppression through some form of censorship is a means of defense, and, speaking broadly, suppression is practiced by the guardians of the state, the church, the family, and property. The support of censorship is to be found among those who feel themselves to be in harmony with the purposes of the institution that is attacked—that is to say, among officials and party workers and the classes who depend most upon the protection of the state, among churchmen and the devout, among parents, teachers, the guardians of the young, among the elderly and the sexually settled, and also among the impotent and inhibited—all those in short whose manner of life would become confused if the particular institution were radically altered. They are the reserves of conservatism from which are mobilized the legions of defense against the irregular forces of the outsiders—the immature, the unprivileged, the unsettled, and the unadjusted, by whom rebellions are made.

The defenders of authority assume that a considerable part of the people, including all children, are not attached by fixed and reliable habits to the existing order. Being unattached they are impressionable, and might therefore be seduced by agitators. They do not have within themselves, inherent in their characters, that interested loyalty to things as they are which makes men immune to subversive influences. In matters of this sort we must remember that the words "right" and "wrong" mean simply friendly or hostile to the purposes of the institution in question; that is why it is said that the outsiders do not have the interest of the institution sufficiently at heart to feel instinctively the difference between right and wrong. They cannot be allowed to judge for themselves because they are without the premises of sound judgment. They are not unconsciously loyal, and their impressions have to be controlled by the insiders who are intuitively right-minded.

The rationalist argument for liberty, as stated for example by Mill, does not meet this powerful dogma squarely. That, it seems to me, is why the stock theories of liberty are persuasive only to the party which is in rebellion and to a few neutrals who are not vitally concerned with the quarrel. The doctrinaires of liberty base their theory on the assumption that almost all men have the ability to weigh evidence and choose reasonably. Whether almost all men have the ability or not, they certainly do not use it. They are governed by their interests as they conceive them by consulting their feelings about them. The men who ever reach a conclusion which is contrary to their bias and their convenience are too few to make any important difference in the course of events. I have taken into account the fact that some men will sacrifice their lives, their fortunes, and their reputations in the pursuit of an ideal or under the compulsion of some deep necessity of which they may not be wholly aware. The hero and the saint would not be so distinguished if their conduct were normal. For the run of men and women, who make up human society, the thing which decides their attitude in a concrete and critical issue is not evidence, argument and repartee, but whether they are attached to or repelled by the institution which is under fire.

The neutrally-minded person with a somewhat liberal disposition often misunderstands this conflict because it does not really touch him. He merely apprehends it as he apprehends the news that forty miners have been trapped in a mine. But your rebel knows his side of the conflict as the doomed miners know their anguish, in a way that a disinterested mind can never know it. The rebel feels his rebellion not as a plea for this or that reform but as an unbearable tension in his viscera. He must break down the cause of his frustration or jump out of his own skin. The true conservative has the same sort of organic need: his institution is to him a mainstay of his being; it exists not as an idea but in the very structure of his character, and the threat to destroy it fills him with anxiety and with fury.

The battles of liberty are organic conflicts between the adjusted and the unadjusted.

March, 1927.

AN ANTICIPATION OF HARDING

IF an optimist is a man who makes lemonade out of all the lemons that are handed to him, then Senator Harding is the greatest of all optimists. He has been told by his friends and his critics that he is colorless and without sap, commonplace and dull, weak and servile. Right you are, says the Senator. You have described exactly the kind of man this country needs. It has tried Roosevelt and Wilson, and look!—it can't stand the gaff. I am nothing that they were. I am no superman like Roosevelt and no superthinker like Wilson. Therefore, I am just the man you are looking for. How do I know that? I am distinguished by the fact that nothing distinguishes me. I am marked for leadership because I have no marks upon me. I am just the man because no one can think of a single reason why I am the man. If any one happens to think of a reason, then I shall cease to be that normal man which these abnormal times demand.

Just what is Mr. Harding trying to say anyway? Presumably some idea is lodged in his brain and panting for utterance beyond the normal human impulse to find a good reason for his own candidacy. For the sake of good appearances in history, I suppose that Mr. Harding is not exalting his defects as do the preternaturally wise animals in Clarence Day's "This Simian World." He can't just be the one-eyed man who is against two-eyed men, or the tortoise who thinks the hare leads too fast a life. Some other idea is sprouting on that front lawn in Marion, Ohio.

That idea, probably, is that the Presidency has grown too big for any man, and that the time has come for decentralizing its power. There are conceivably two ways this might be done. One way would be to think out a plan for adapting responsible cabinet government to the congressional system. It is a way that would require an abnormal lot of thinking. It would require also a quarrel with Congress. For until Congress disgorges its petty control over the details of administration, Congress will not be fit to take upon itself major control of executive policy. But Congress at present is so much concerned with the things that do not belong to it, that it has no opportunity to be concerned with the things that do. The relation of Congress to administration is like that of a general staff so tremendously interested in the second lieutenants that it ignores the lieutenant generals. The result is that the generals can't command the lieutenants, and the lieutenants' hair is forever standing on end while they try to obey the swivel chairs. Mr. Harding's remedy for this is to sack the general and find some one who will be content with his four stars and keep his mouth shut.

There is something in it. If you can't think of any way to redistribute the functions of government, then all you have to do is to find a President who will be so weak that power will leave him. That is the inner meaning of Mr. Harding's nomination. He was put there by the Senators for the sole purpose of abdicating in their favor. The Grand Dukes have chosen their weak Tsar in order to increase the power of the Grand Dukes. And if he is elected the period will be known in our constitutional history as the Regency of the Senate.

What will this accomplish? It will reduce the prestige and the power of the White House. Will it create a better balance of prestige and power in the whole government? Hardly. The gentlemen who intend to benefit by Mr. Harding's abnormal normality are a group tiny enough to meet in a hotel bedroom. They are not the elected Congress of the United States. Their rise to power would mean not the restoration of a balance between executive and legislature but the substitution of government by a clique for the lonely majesty of the President. Dangerous as is the plight we are in, it has at least the advantage of visibility. The President may be an autocrat, yet every one knows where that autocrat lives. But the government of a clique, an invisible, self-invited collection of friends, would be just nothing but the return of exactly what every decent person has fought against for a generation.

That the glory of the normal should be presented to a weary nation as the purest Republican doctrine according to the Fathers is one of those paradoxes which, Mr. Chesterton says, always sit beside the wells of truth. It is in fact primitive Democratic doctrine. That doctrine has always been that anybody could govern, that leadership was dangerous, excellence somewhat un-American, and specialized knowledge somewhat sinister. The Republicans from Hamilton's time on have always professed a belief that ability mattered, and that no system of government could succeed in which the best men were not preëminent. They may have had some queer notions about what constituted the best men, but they have at least done this republic the service of refusing to accept the idea that anybody could do anything. They have not in theory at least stooped to encourage the democratic vices. Mr. Harding does. I hate to say it, but he is in ultimate theory a great deal closer to Mr. Bryan than he is to any

great Republican from Hamilton to Root.   For
Mr. Bryan has the same simple faith that any
deserving fellow can do anything, which Mr.
Harding has now brought forth from the caverns
of his mind.

July, 1920.

AN EARLY ESTIMATE OF MR. McADOO

I F the Republicans do not nominate a man who can interest the people now voting for Johnson, and if the Democrats nominate McAdoo, it will be a hot summer for the Republican candidates; and about September fifteenth Mr. Will Hays will begin to sleep badly. For McAdoo is a little like Lloyd George. He knows not only what the owners of votes are thinking now, but what they will be excited about a few weeks from now. He has the political sense: he mobilized his war psychology before most people, and he demobilized it before the rest. He has the gift, which Roosevelt had and Wood lacks, of feeling with, but just ahead, of the mass of the voters; in short, the gift of popular sympathy. He is possessed by what he feels, and men possessed in politics are infectious. Of all candidates he has incomparably the greatest sensibility to the prevailing winds of public opinion. Johnson, who is no mean politician himself, is by comparison immovable because more elemental; Wood is torpid and Lowden contracted and Hoover detached and deductive, but McAdoo is swift to note and swift to move.

He picks his course quickly, moves fast upon it and with great audacity. It may not be quite true, as one interviewer claims, that Secretary McAdoo made eight or nine important decisions one day going down in the elevator of a building in Washington, but it is in the general direction of the truth. He is an agile man. He does not hesitate or brood or procrastinate or reflect at length. Instinctively he prefers the bold and the decisive to the prudent and tepid course, for he is a statesman grafted upon a promoter. The man described as the entrepreneur in the economic textbooks is, I think, the basic McAdoo, the kind of man who really likes enterprises more than profit, organizes ideas, and anticipates wants. That kind of man is first "sold" himself on an idea and then "sells" others. What he is determined to do he is passionately determined to do, once he falls into his stride. He said in 1915, when addressing the Chamber of Commerce of the United States at Washington in advocacy of the Shipping Bill:

"Since I have come to Washington there is one word in the English language with which I have become more familiar than any other, because it is

the one word that is used most. I say that advisedly.
I use it myself too much, and every time I use it I
get ashamed of myself. You can talk to any man
about anything and the first thing he says is, 'I'm
afraid of so-and-so and so-and-so.' He is afraid of
something. Where is the courage of the American nation? Where is that virile power that has
made this American nation great? Has it disap-
peared? I do not believe it. We are not afraid of
anything, my friends, so long as we walk the path of
rectitude and justice as a nation, and we intend to
do that; and if this shipping bill passes all this talk
about getting into international difficulties is mere
twaddle."

There are, I imagine, things of which McAdoo is
afraid but they are not the usual spooks which
terrify public officials. He is not afraid of responsibility, nor of dinner-table gossip, nor of congressional investigation, nor of private talk, nor of
editorial writers, nor of experiment. Above all he
is not afraid of words. He is remarkably free of
the clatter made by rusty old tin-can words like
reactionary, radical, socialist.

"I believe there is no intelligent banker, business
man or citizen of this country, who understands the
Federal Reserve system and its workings, who does
not thank God for the great law which created that

system whether it be socialistic or whether it puts the government into the banking business or not." (October 13, 1915, before the Chamber of Commerce of Indianapolis.)

He had fought for that system and had helped to make it, he was for it, he was "sold," and he was prepared to thank God for it, and make a monkey of any one from Senator Root down who had opposed it. When McAdoo is under way he treats them rough, as almost any Republican candidate would quickly discover. He will not stand on ceremony. If he thinks miners are underpaid, if he sees the government muddling, he will not hesitate to call the public's attention to the statistics of profits which exist for public use in Senate document No. 259, 65th Congress, 2d Session.

In that famous instance he did no more than quote figures which over a year and a quarter had been public property, but he will not play an insider's game as the insider plays it. He has not the normal reticence and inhibitions of finance and politics. By experience as well as temperament he is an outsider who knows the inside wires. He is disposed at critical moments to tell more than is usually told, even at the risk of inconveniencing a few people and of scandalizing many. McAdoo is distinctly not a safe person in the ordinary sense of the word. He is less safe than most devout progressives because he is so clever and so sophisticated. He has a devilish knowledge of the tender spots, and a willingness to touch them occasionally.

What restrains him is not etiquette, nor the sentiments of the best people, nor fear of novelty, nor the compulsions of routine and tradition. He is not organized by a class feeling, nor by a set of profoundly imbedded general principles. He is organized by a remarkable sense of what a governing majority of voters wants and will receive. He is aware of himself and of the political possibilities. He is bold to seize the possibilities, but prudent not to overstep them. He is not a gambler and not a fanatic and not an evangelical reformer. He is a projector of concrete programs, and a promoter who can reveal to people that those programs embody what they already desire. He is an administrator of the first order. McAdoo is a man who makes his way in the world, not by conformity but by initiative, not by pull or by regularity or even by genius, but by his wits. He is the kind of man who is self-made several times over. He is big, at any rate, in two dimensions. He has length and breadth if not depth.

The defects of his virtues are revealed rather clearly in the statements he issued some months ago about the finances of the government. There was a cry at that time to the effect that posterity should pay a larger portion of the costs of the war. The cry has served as General Wood's financial religion ever since, although on second thought people are beginning to think differently. McAdoo was caught by the gust.

"I think the present generation could with perfect propriety hand on to posterity the ultimate settlement of that part of our debt which remains unliquidated."

And therefore he proposed a highly ingenious scheme of funding and postponing, coupled with a plan to buy Jamaica, the Bahamas, Barbados, Nassau, British Honduras, and the Bermudas, with the British obligations. In public office such a stunt would probably not emanate from McAdoo, for he has the faculty of surrounding himself with excellent men. The proposal was prestidigitated out of private life, but it illustrates one aspect of the free play of his mind. It originated in a superficial public opinion of which he was acutely aware, and it was fertilized by a clever imagination. But it was not governed by sustained conviction about the enduring obligations and needs of a democratic people. It was facile and it was bold, but not calculated to produce the profoundest confidence.

I have deliberately selected what seems to me the worst example I can find. It is probably not typical, but it is an exaggerated symptom to be noted. Mr. McAdoo has been a truly distinguished public servant. When the smoke of manufactured opinions clears away, his administration of the railroads will probably be regarded as a piece of heroic and successful intervention in one of the worst crises of the war. There are not many who can estimate the work of any Secretary of the Treasury, and I am not one of them. But I have heard observers who were detached, had a chance to know, and knew how to know, rate McAdoo very high among Treasury officials. There is really no question of the practical competence of McAdoo. There is no more question of it than there is of Hoover's. Both are remarkable organizers and remarkable executives.

The doubt about McAdoo is really the obverse of the doubt about Hoover. Personally Hoover is extraordinarily fine and sensitive, but politically he has shown himself to be secluded and unaware. Lacking stimulation from the mass, he deduces opinions from a few stock ideas in any political situation where his energy is not focused by a specific task. McAdoo is less intricate personally, but infinitely more sensitive to the stimulus of popular feeling. When he misjudges that feeling, as of course he must occasionally, or when the important thing is not popular feeling but the governing idea of a situation beyond the scope of immediate practical application, then McAdoo is likely to be quite conventional and rhetorical, and flat, and catering. His speeches on foreign affairs, especially in the early stages of the Treaty debate, are of this order. On the Fourth of July, 1919, for example, he was arguing for the Treaty: "Separate the League of Nations from the Treaty and it would be utterly impossible to enforce the Treaty. . . ." That was the time, July, 1919, when nobody had read the Treaty and everybody liked it because it was hard on the Huns. A year later Mr. McAdoo was saying something to the effect that God won the war but the devil won the peace. There had been the beginning of a radical change in public opinion. A beginning was enough. A hint is enough for McAdoo, but he needs the hint.

Thus in recent interviews he has been courageous and straightforward on contentious questions affecting civil liberty, Russia, the Palmer injunction, and the whole paraphernalia of the Red hysteria. He has talked the way free men are supposed to talk about these things. But he was not among the first to protest, because he is not fundamentally moved by the simple moralities. He is liberal but worldly, he is bold but immediate, he is brave but not selfless. He would win many skirmishes, and make brilliant dashes, and achieve some victories, but for the long strategic campaigning of democracy, it is hard to tell about him.

June, 1920.

WILSON AND HOUSE

I

THESE two volumes [1] tell Colonel House's story of his association with Woodrow Wilson through the period of American neutrality. They end with a scene at the White House after the delivery of the war message; the President, his family, and the Colonel are alone together.

The two friends had spent the day doing nothing except kill time until the President was called to the Capitol. House set down in his diary that he could see signs of nervousness beneath the President's apparent calm. "In the morning he told me he was determined not to speak after three o'clock, believing it would make a bad impression—an impression that he was unduly pressing matters. I thought differently and persuaded him that he should hold

[1] "The Intimate Papers of Colonel House." Arranged as a narrative by Charles Seymour. Vol. I. Behind the Political Curtain, 1912-1915. Vol. II. From Neutrality to War, 1915-1917.

himself ready to address Congress whenever that body indicated their readiness to hear him. It turned out that he began to speak at twenty minutes to nine and finished in about thirty-two minutes. I timed him carefully." . . . It was like the two men, the one in such an agony of doubt over the awful responsibility of the decision into which he had been pushed that he snatched at a pretext that might allow him to delay; the other imperturbable and aware of the immediate requirements of the occasion even to setting down in his diary that he had timed the President carefully and that he spoke about thirty-two minutes. Colonel House did not put down in his diary that night how he felt about the entry of the United States into a great European war, except to say that it seemed to him that "Wilson did not have a true conception of the path he was blazing." It was House's business to be calm and so he simply wrote that they had dined early, at half past six, and that they talked of everything except the matter in hand, that when they returned from the Capitol the family gathered in the Oval Room, where House showed Wilson a clipping from some paper, and said to Wilson he was like Mazzini. "I could see the President was relieved that the tension was over and the die cast. I knew this would happen."

Even if the two men had not had such different temperaments, they would have felt differently on that fateful day. To Wilson the declaration of war was the tragic failure of his own hopes; to House it was a step to which he was thoroughly adjusted, for he had long regarded war as probable, as necessary, and as a great opportunity. Wilson hated the decision with all his soul; for about two weeks he fought the matter out in his own mind, absolutely alone. As late as the day before he went to Congress he told Frank Cobb of his horror and cried out to him: "If there is any alternative, for God's sake, let's take it!" House, on the other hand, was not beset by these doubts. He remained in New York during Wilson's agony, and did not go to Washington till the decision was made. He found when Wilson showed him the text of the message that "no address he has yet made pleases me more than this one."

Although they were associated so closely, it is evident that these two men felt very differently about the war. Wilson, in spite of the complexity of his character and his mind, was moved by the old American feeling that America is a new land which must not be entangled with Europe. The sympathy of his mind was pro-Allies though chastened by a certain irony about their moral pretensions, a suspicion of their motives, and a conviction that unfortunately they too were mad; in this period his heart was always neutral and non-European. His real judgment he expressed several times, to the horror not only of the Allied spokesmen but of Colonel House; it was that the war arose out of obscure causes that were hatched in a sinister system and a tortuous

diplomacy. Wilson never accepted the official propaganda even when it blew the hottest; he never
respected it, and could hardly bear to listen to it.
What he wanted above all things was to keep out
of the hideous mess. House, on the other hand, was
much too practical a politician to permit himself to
stray into such a wilderness of unusable truth, even
if he had not really wanted the Allies to win. House
wanted those very things to which Wilson ultimately
gave his official consent and about half his soul's
desire. He did not share Wilson's reluctance and
foreboding, and he appears in these volumes, perhaps a little more consistently than he was in fact,
as the protagonist of what might be called the
British liberal imperialist view as against the
instinctive American isolationist view of Woodrow
Wilson.

Unfortunately this record does not contain Wilson's side of the correspondence with House, nor of
course any account of Wilson's feelings about their
relationship. It is like listening to one side of a
broken conversation on the telephone, and not quite
even that, for the record we have is what House put
down and Mr. Seymour selected. It is plain to me,
however, from House's letters that he did not press
very hard on their differences, and that their association was friendly but careful. There are hints
occasionally which lead one to think that Wilson
would not have tolerated urgency from House or
from any one else. Thus in these papers Mr. Sey-

mour gives great weight to a letter written by House to Wilson on July 19, 1915, in which he says: "If war comes with Germany, it will be because of our unpreparedness and her belief that we are more or less impotent to do her harm." But there is no evidence that House ever made an issue of this crucial matter, nor that he gave it the emphasis at the time which Mr. Seymour gives it by quoting the sentence at the head of Chapter I of the second volume.

I am inclined to believe, therefore, that although this was the closest political friendship of Woodrow Wilson's life, it was a friendship at some distance and always of a certain fragility. Wilson told House more than he told his Cabinet, and certainly no other adviser in this period had so much of his confidence. But there were reservations, and there does not seem ever to have been the intimacy of two friends who can say anything to each other without misunderstanding. The letters are friendly, but they are the letters of one statesman to another. They leave me feeling that House had to consider carefully how he would approach Wilson.

House had a more coherent, even if it was a simpler, view of the war and of the part he wished Wilson to play; he was not tormented by Wilson's hatred of war, by his dreadful sense that victory is a snare, by his desire to wrench himself free from the encompassing of a tragic fate. House was business-like about the business at hand, and did not look long into the bottomless pit; thought and feeling and the action he recommended were worldly and of a piece. But in Wilson there was an unworldliness of pity and doubt and high contempt that prevented him from agreeing wholly with much that circumstances forced him to do. The figure of Wilson is dim in these pages, but here and there we catch a glimpse of him as he struggles very much alone against the advancing chaos. Now and then the real future is illuminated for him by a flash of insight. But these prophecies only cause him anguish, for they show him how different is the path he is compelled to take from that which he thinks he ought to take.

II

Colonel House served the President in many different rôles—as friend, adviser, scout, observer, secret agent, political manipulator, negotiator, and sifter of information and opinion. But his main task was to accommodate the personal attitude of Wilson to the exigencies of the war. For Wilson stood aloof not only from its detail but from the official premises and official criteria of his time. He wished to keep the country out of the war. For that reason he wished to end the war. He did not wish to fight in order merely to vindicate that part of our neutral rights which Germany was violating. If he had to fight, he wished to justify war by some objective which was greater than the war aims of the Allies.

The aloofness of Wilson from the pressure of those who usually surround the head of a state helped him to his uncanny understanding of what the mass of American people really believed about the war. It is no wonder they reëlected him in 1916 in the belief that he had kept the country out of the war in Europe, nor that they elected the Republicans in 1920 because they promised to keep the country out of Europe and another war in Europe. In the period of neutrality Wilson saw more clearly than any living man what the country really wanted. He was in sympathy with the country. He was very much alone, and yet his intuitions were those of the mass of unseen and non-vocal Americans, once you looked below the views which were acquired and imposed by German frightfulness and Allied propaganda and the personal and social connections of the upper classes on the Eastern seaboard.

Colonel House, too, had a certain initial American suspicion of Europe, but he was a much more sociable man than Wilson, and he was at once more trustful of, and more sensitive to, the upper officialized opinion. He became in a sense the honest broker between Wilson, who longed for peace without entanglement, and the people on both sides of the Atlantic who had set themselves to draw the United States into the war. The formula which House evolved first during his negotiations with Grey in London early in 1916 became later the Wilson policy of a war to found a League of Nations; it was at bottom a compromise formula to satisfy both Wilson's instincts and the demands of the pro-Allies. House proposed to buy the assent of the Allies to a conference to end the war by offering to enter the war on the side of the Allies if Germany refused the conference or insisted upon a victorious peace. As I read the record, Wilson never fully agreed to this proposal in so far as it involved a promise to enter the war. But he did take from it the principle that American influence should be used as a makeweight against aggression and a stabilizer of peace. Thus it came about that when he entered the war, he did not think of himself as primarily engaged in a war against Germany on the side of the Allies. He thought he was using the force of the United States to tame Germany and to restrain the Allies in order that there might be established a permanent conference to prevent war.

In these volumes we see the origins of what came to be known as the Wilson policy. We can see how the President began to formulate an ideal future as the pressure of events forced him into a course of action which he detested. And in it all Colonel House appears as the man who suggested to Wilson how he could do, in a way which nearly satisfied his conscience, what immeasurably great events were compelling him against his will to do. A psychologist might say that House supplied Wilson with the rationalizations by means of which Wilson was able to bow to a destiny that was overbearing him, and even ultimately to sow the seed of a triumph that may make him immortal.

III

The machinery by which Colonel House kept in touch with the war was so simple that it might be called primitive. He had direct contact with Grey at the British Foreign Office and with Bernstorff. He had only a casual contact with the French Government or with the Italian or the Russian. He had access, of course, to what the State Department could learn about the war, but that was admittedly not much from the point of view of high politics. He had a useful and illuminating correspondence with Gerard at Berlin, and much less illuminating correspondence with other American Ambassadors. He went to England, Germany, and France several times and had interviews with the leading statesmen. But when all is said and done, it was with the British alone, and then only with a certain section of the British, and with this section not in fullest confidence, that he had a continuous discussion.

With Grey at the British Foreign Office he used a secret code; he had the closest personal contact with the head of the British Secret Service in America, and by this means a channel of communication was opened which passed by the British Embassy in Washington, the State Department, and the American Embassy in London. He had no comparable relations with any of the other Allies, and with the Germans he had only a friendly but cautious contact with Bernstorff, who was himself considerably an outsider in the conduct of foreign policy. His friendships in Britain were with men like Grey, Bryce, Plunkett, and to a certain extent Balfour, but there is no evidence that they told him all they knew, or all that he had under the circumstances perhaps a fair right to know. And it is plain that the imperial statesmen like Curzon, and Lloyd George himself, and Milner, and the permanent but dominating Foreign Office, were outside the orbit of House, and quite content to leave the persuasion of Wilson and House to those British liberals who most nearly talked the language that Americans understand.

The objective proof of this is to be found in the fact that although House negotiated with Grey in 1916, making a tentative offer to enter the war on the side of the Allies, Grey never explained to House that the Allies were bound to each other by a series of secret treaties that made acceptance of Wilson's conditions impossible. Grey's letter to House explaining his moral scruples about considering the offer is one of the least informing documents that any one could have written under the circumstances. There is no doubt that the negotiations of 1916 were conducted in the dark, and that neither Wilson nor House seems to have known fully the inner diplomatic history of those days. Mr. Seymour in a footnote (Vol. I, p. 443) states that Mr. Balfour explained the details of the Italian Treaty to President Wilson on April 30, 1917. That was rather late in the day. Nobody explained that treaty or any other to House when he was in London discussing so important a matter as the entrance of the United States into the war. It is impossible, therefore, to feel that even so able a man as House, with so great a gift as his for friendships, is even a partially adequate substitute for an effective diplomatic service.

IV

The secret negotiations of February, 1916, were the most important diplomatic effort that House undertook in the period covered by these volumes. The conclusions of a conference on February 14 were embodied in a memorandum written by Sir Edward Grey which is dated February 22. The substance of the proposal as made by House is as follows:

"Colonel House told me that President Wilson was ready, on hearing from France and England that the moment was opportune, to propose that a conference should be summoned to put an end to the war. Should the Allies accept this proposal and should Germany refuse it, the United States would enter the war against Germany.

"Colonel House expressed the opinion that, if

such a conference met, it would secure peace on terms
not unfavorable to the Allies; and if it failed to
secure peace, the United States would leave the conference as a belligerent on the side of the Allies, if
Germany was unreasonable. . . ."

That is the way the proposal read when House
left London. On March 6, he arrived in Washington and went over the memorandum with
President Wilson. Two days later, on March 8,
Wilson wrote a telegram to Grey for House to
sign which read as follows:

"I reported to the President the general conclusions of our conference of the 14th of February,
and in the light of those conclusions he authorizes
me to say that, so far as he can speak for the future
actions of the United States, he agrees to the memorandum with which you have furnished me, with
only this correction: that the word 'probably' be
added after the word 'would' and before the word
'leave' in line number nine."

Thus, after Wilson had amended it, the proposal
read that "the United States would *probably* enter
the war against Germany," and not that "the United
States would enter the war against Germany"; that
"the United States would *probably* leave the conference as a belligerent" and not that "the United
States would leave it as a belligerent." In a foot-

note to the account of this incident (Vol. II, p. 21)
Mr. Seymour says that:

"The value of the offer was in no way lessened by
the use of the word 'probably,' which was a conventional covering expression common in diplomatic
documents. Since the power to declare war resides
in Congress and since the President shares with the
Senate the control of foreign policy, it would have
been impossible for Wilson to give a categorical
guaranty of the future actions of the United States.
As a matter of practice, however, the President can
determine the question of peace and war, and the
expression of his intention appears here in the
strongest permissible form."

It is hard for me to believe that the British Foreign Office in 1916 interpreted the insertion of the
word "probably" as Mr. Seymour interprets it in
1925. Assuming that British statesmen understood
the subtleties of our constitutional system, it seems
to me that they must nevertheless have regarded the
President's use of the word "probably" as a reservation on the President's own action as well as on that
of Congress. The President did not say categori-
cally: "I will recommend to Congress that the
United States enter the war," as he might have
done if that was what he was intending to do. The
use of the word "probably" reserved liberty of action
for Wilson, and so the Allies must have understood

it. It must be remembered that at the very time these secret negotiations were in progress, the President was being reviled in the pro-Allied press of America and Europe as pro-German, pacifist and spineless; and that just before House talked to Grey, the State Department accepted publicly, though temporarily, the German position on the arming of merchant vessels. I do not see how it is possible to suppose that the Allies took the word "probably" as a "conventional covering expression," and not as a weasel word which radically altered the sense of the House proposal.

Once you reject Mr. Seymour's explanation and take the Wilson amendment as meaning what it appears to say, you arrive at this result: *House* proposed a conference which would either obtain moderate terms for the Allies or American assistance in the war; *Wilson*, on the other hand, proposed a conference to end the war with no commitment that he would even try to enter the war if the conference failed. I do not believe that House and Wilson clearly understood each other here; in this incident we can see that in spite of their apparent agreement they started from different premises about the war, and that their minds worked differently as to the American objective. It is necessary to add that there is every reason to think that the Allies had a truer realization of Wilson's attitude than House who, in the stress of working for a great plan, did not distinguish sharply between what he hoped would happen and what President Wilson wished to have happen.

If Mr. Seymour's interpretation were correct the incident would be a crucial one in the history of the war and in the history of American politics. As yet we have only two versions, that of Colonel House, and the gracious but highly officialized account of Lord Grey's "Twenty-Five Years." (Vol. II, p. 126 *et seq.*) We do not know Wilson's version, and we do not know what the Allied statesmen thought of it all. We do know enough to be wary of Mr. Seymour's definite verdict that "House had shown them how, by merely raising a beckoning hand, they might have the assurance either of a peace of justice or a victory won with American assistance." (Vol. II, p. 203.) The implied charge against the Allied statesmen is a very grave one, and no doubt in the course of time they will answer it.

If Mr. Seymour were right, the matter would be no less grave from the point of view of America. For he insists that a President of the United States offered in secret to commit this country to enter a war in order to achieve a certain diplomatic settlement in Europe. For myself I do not believe that there is any evidence that Woodrow Wilson did anything of the kind, and I am personally convinced that the incident is much simpler to interpret than Mr. Seymour's version implies. I give my own interpretation for what it is worth, recalling again that we do not know the whole story. I think Wilson wished above all to avoid war. I think he would have been willing to have almost any peace in Europe if he could keep America out of war. I think he saw that if once he could induce the belligerents to begin talking that they never could resume fighting. He was willing to try any device, including the House negotiations, that might bring on a conference, *provided* it did not commit him to entering the war. And I think that is exactly the sense in which the Allies understood it, and that is exactly why they ignored it. They had no promise from Wilson that really counted. And in a conference at that time their divergence of aims would have come to the surface, the secret treaties would have seriously damaged their moral standing, and the coalition might have broken up. Finally and above all they knew that if they maintained their blockade, Germany would either starve or resume submarine warfare. If Germany starved, Wilson's restraining influence would be eliminated in the peace conference; if Germany resumed warfare, Wilson would be driven to enter the war without conditions.

If this interpretation is correct, the negotiations were a failure not because the Allies were too stupid to seize a great opportunity, as Mr. Seymour suggests, or too high-minded, as Lord Grey suggests. The negotiations failed because Wilson had nothing to negotiate with: he would promise nothing and he would threaten nothing. He would not promise to go to war with Germany and he would not threaten to enforce American rights against the Allies. The offer inspired neither hope nor fear. And when empires are at war it is not possible to deflect them with insubstantial proposals.

V

And yet out of these same negotiations grew that advocacy of a League of Nations which may yet cause Woodrow Wilson to be numbered among the great benefactors of mankind. As Wilson understood the House-Grey negotiations they were an attempt to provoke a conference, end the war, and thus extricate the United States from an otherwise insoluble difficulty. The failure of these negotiations seems to have made clear to Wilson that the United States was caught in circumstances which allowed it no escape from the fate of the rest of the world. During the spring which followed the winter's failure he seems finally to have concluded that neutrality was untenable for the United States in a great war, and that the philosophy of isolation would have to be revised. He still fought against the practical consequences and hoped that he might avoid participation in this war. But he realized that as the world grew more and more interdependent no succeeding President would be able to maintain neutrality even as long as he had.

It was with a foreboding that even he might not be able to escape that he publicly espoused the idea

of a League of Nations in his great speech of
May 27, 1916. He had then come to the conclusion
that if he was forced into the war all he could hope
to obtain as compensation for such immeasurable
evil was an organized peace. Wilson was determined
not to fight a war merely for American neutral rights
as against the submarine. For he realized that those
rights could not be vindicated by war, and the event
has fully borne him out. The treaty of peace does
not in any way mention the rights of neutrals against
submarines and the submarine to-day is exactly the
same instrument of frightfulness as it was in 1917.
When the victory was won and peace was made, the
victorious Allies did not trouble even to pass a resolution against submarines. Wilson felt that to enter
the war merely for the sake of our rights would not
be worth the suffering and the cost.

He set himself, therefore, the noble task of establishing some permanent benefit as the objective in
case the United States was forced into the war. It
was in that way, if I read the record rightly, that
he turned to the League of Nations. Other men
before him had advocated the idea. The greatness
of Wilson lay in his prophetic understanding that
this was the one good he might be able to promote
and defend in the face of the oncoming disaster. It
was the one compensation, it was the one reasonable
ideal, it was the one moral justification, it was the
one balm to his conscience for the plunging of a
great people into the red madness of Europe.

If Wilson had prepared for the ordeal of war in practice as he prepared for it in principle, his claim to supreme greatness among statesmen would not be open to dispute. But the record of these memoirs shows that he and House up to 1917 were dependent for their knowledge of the war largely upon what belligerent statesmen chose to tell them. They had no secret service and no diplomatic service which could inform them either as to the secret engagements or the secret purposes of the European governments. And they never learned before the declaration of war that there were in existence solemn and binding agreements which were bound in large measure to prevent the making of such a just and conciliatory settlement as they needed for the foundation of a successful League of Nations. Therefore, they missed the golden opportunity of exacting pledges from the Allies for an American peace. The Allies had to buy the help of Rumania and of Italy. But they got American help for nothing, and by that disastrous oversight the whole grand purpose of Wilson was almost wrecked at Paris.

VI

The fame of House will depend of course upon the fame of Wilson, just as Wilson's fame will depend upon the success of the League of Nations. House, it seems to me, is bound to share in whatever fame Wilson finally achieves, for it is evident even

from the scanty records available that he helped
more than any other man, and that he helped deci-
sively, to commit Wilson to the cause of the League.
It seems to me of slight consequence whether or not
the fulsome judgments of his biographer are
accepted by posterity. Even the claims of the
biographer which are bound to embarrass the
Colonel's friends are of little permanent importance.

Time, and a sense of reality, and a fuller knowledge, will change the perspective in which these
letters and diaries are set, and there will emerge, I
feel sure, in place of the picture of a man who
directed destiny, the picture of a man who stood
faithfully at Wilson's side against a destiny that
overwhelmed them both, but in that vain and often
blind resistance did help to kindle a light for the
generations to come.

April, 1926.

BORAH

I

I N due course Senator Borah has been made Chairman of the Committee on Foreign Relations. He has come into this high estate not by election of the people or by choice of his own party but under the rule of seniority. He has outlasted his predecessors. I mention this fact because it establishes his independence at the outset. A man who has attained an office because he is alive and because he continues to be elected by the people of

Idaho is under no great compulsion to regard himself as the mere mouthpiece of a President or of a Secretary of State. *Deo volente,* he will survive them both. If only he continues to eat moderately, to exercise regularly, to sleep well, and to keep about half the voters in the State of Idaho on his side, he can look with cool detachment on any suggestion that issues from the White House.

The ordinary inducements to conformity count for little in Mr. Borah's case. There are many more voters on the island of Manhattan alone than in the whole State of Idaho; with such a small constituency to nurse Senator Borah does not have to worry about the favors and threats of the national administration. His constituency is manageable. He can really talk to it and make a direct personal contact with the local leaders who dispose of votes. No wonder his faith in an appeal to the people is unshaken, for there are so few people to whom he has to make his appeal. A loyal following of less than seventy-five thousand voters in Idaho is enough to make his reëlection certain. Mr. Borah does not need to worry. A national administration cannot help or hurt him much.

But he can help or hurt the administration. He is the greatest figure in the Northwest, and the Northwest is about as warmly attached to the Republican Party as the Irish Free State is to the United Kingdom. The Northwest votes Republican in presidential years, and then forms a coalition with the Democrats against almost all major Republican policies. President Coolidge and the Republicans of the East know that there are good reasons for being very kind to Senator Borah. For although he has never actually run away as Roosevelt did in 1912, there is something about him which suggests that he might. He is allowed to go his own way, therefore, in the reasonable hope that if he is given enough space in which to roam about within the party, he will find it convenient to stay inside the party.

Thus it has come to pass that wholly domestic considerations have given Mr. Borah a peculiar independence in international affairs.

II

He exercises the power of protest and of veto. It is a power exactly suited to his temperament. For Senator Borah has little interest in what is usually called constructive statesmanship. He is not possessed by a desire to make two institutions grow where one grew before. He does not like and he does not trust officials and committees and administrative hierarchies and executive orders and large payrolls and pensions. When some one comes to him with a proposal for elaborating the machinery of society, be it to maintain peace, to protect children, or to pension and instruct mothers, it is no lack of interest in the object but a congenital dislike of the machinery which brings him finally into opposition. Borah was born and bred on the frontier far from the complexity of modern civilization; it is in his bones to distrust formality and collective red tape, and to rely upon direct speech, common knowledge, individual salvation and his own conception of the sovereign power of the moral law. The strain of Jefferson, and of Rousseau, of the Reformers before them, runs strongly in Borah. He believes in the natural goodness of man, and, when that goodness is deficient, in the natural right of man to be damned in his own way. Thus recently he wrote to me, quoting Buckle, that "the most valuable additions made to legislation have been enactments destructive of preceding legislation." The real business of the statesman, in his philosophy, is not to construct institutions for the regimentation of men but to tear down those vested follies of the ages which thwart the natural goodness of mankind. Therefore, when Borah considers a new proposal he does not ask himself: What does this add to the machinery of living? Borah asks himself: Does it subtract from a machinery which is already top-heavy? Thus, the word "constructive" casts no spell upon him; he has read history with a deeply protestant mind and has concluded that what statesmen have usually constructed is a prison house for the soul.

It follows inevitably that the career of Borah is built upon opposition. He has been against the

League, and against the Court, and against the
Pacific Pact, and against the British funding arrangements, and against the Wilson-Hughes Russian
policy, and against the Caribbean policy, and against
the Isle of Pines Treaty, and against the exclusion
of Count Karolyi and Mr. Saklatvala, and against
the alien property administration, and against the
bonus, and against the Child Labor Amendment,
and against Coolidge Republicanism, and against
LaFollette insurgency. He is an instinctive conscientious objector, and his mind seizes swiftly upon
the reasons why anything that is about to be done
should not be done. His passion is to expose, to
ventilate, to protest, to prevent and to destroy.
Since he does not have a hankering to create institutions, pass laws, or facilitate agreements, he has no
use for the reticences and frustrations that are
required in public affairs. Thus, for example, he
was once arguing with Senator Brandegee that
treaties should be discussed publicly in the Senate,
and Mr. Brandegee had made the point that too
much plain speech might give offense to foreign
countries. "What are these delicate questions,"
retorted Senator Borah, "which may offend foreign
powers? These delicate questions are too often
questions of dubious righteousness." Only a man
who has risen by appealing to audiences rather than
by making executive decisions would, I think, have
said that.

III

Now ordinarily such a man would find himself extremely unpopular in a country where the passion for doing something, or even anything, is so highly regarded. He would be labeled a chronic kicker and dismissed from the society of the righteous and the efficient.

That has not been Senator Borah's fate. It may be that he has lost a little in prestige since he became the Chairman of the Committee on Foreign Relations. Many people say he has, but I am not so sure they are right. For they are the same people who think that the whole term of Mr. Coolidge will be like the present honeymoon when nobody is seriously dissatisfied with anything. It is in the nature of things that a great protestant like Borah should lose lustre in a time of fabulous complacency and contentment. But as surely as there will be new causes for discontent, so there will be a revival of Borah's influence. For in the existing confusion and paralysis of the Democratic Party he is the natural rallying point of the opposition.

In America to-day any one who is out of sorts with anything thinks first of Mr. Borah. That is why he has grown great on opposition rather than weak by his chronic objecting. Within the last few years most of the large blocs of voters have been more deeply opposed to something than they have been

eager for anything. The internationally minded
wanted the League and the Court but Borah touched
their hearts by his outspoken oppostion to the Ruhr,
his attitude toward Russia, Haiti, and China. The
strong nationalists deplored Borah's affection for the
under-dog nations, but where could they find a
champion comparable to him in their fight against
coöperation with Europe? He delighted the
upper classes in the East with his attack on the
bonus, and he delighted the people of the West by
his attack on the international bankers who desire
an easy settlement of the debts. He opposed the
Child Labor Amendment and pleased the conservatives, and he opposed the suppression of free speech
and pleased the liberals. Mr. Borah has not become
an outcast like most objectors because he has made
common cause at one time or another with every
influential group.

On whichever side he fights he is a host in himself,
and those who have had him as their champion in
one cause readily forgive him for all the pet projects
of theirs which he has brought to nothing. Borah is
a very inspiring man to have on one's own side of
the argument. He knows what is theatrically effective, he has an air of common sense, a resourceful-
ness, and an eloquence, which have made him the
most successful debater in the Senate. He has a
still greater quality than these. Borah's opposition
has no poison in it. For some subtle reason, Borah
does not make enemies of his opponents. One would

expect that a man who had fought everybody's
dearest project at one time or another would be
hated throughout the land. Borah is not hated anywhere. On the contrary there is not a gathering
from a bankers' convention to a communist meeting
where Borah is not respected. He was the one
irreconcilable enemy of the League with whom the
friends of the League were on friendly terms. He
has opposed almost everybody and has embittered
nobody.

This is due in part to the liking which every one
feels for a man who is known to be brave, in part
also to his vitality and his poise, and to the sense
that he is not bitten and driven by jealousies and
animosities. There is a natural well-ventilated
health in Borah which distinguishes him from the
run of overfed, tobacco-laden, anecdotal indoor
politicians. But there is also a deeper ground of
confidence. Borah's opposition has nothing exotic
about it. He is not against this or that because he
believes in strange doctrines. When a man denies
he also affirms, and Borah always affirms the oldest
American traditions and the simplest popular prejudices. He believes in helping the under-dog, in
distrusting powerful foreigners, in distrusting politicians, in preserving the Constitution, and in holding
on to the taxpayers' money. When Borah is in
opposition to the Child Labor Amendment nobody
thinks he wishes to exploit children; when he opposes
the League nobody thinks he is a militarist and a

jingo; when he opposes the Haitian occupation nobody supposes he has fallen in love with the Haitians; and when he pleads for Russia, *mirabile dictu,* nobody, not even the most furious patrioteer, thinks he is in the pay of Moscow. He has fought the battle of the jingo and the pacifist, the reactionary and the radical, and yet he has not merged his identity with any of them.

IV

It would not occur to Senator Borah, I think, that he must sacrifice any of his liberty of action because he had become Chairman of the Committee on Foreign Relations. He has always spoken his mind on all subjects, and he continues to speak it. If he does not like French policy in Morocco, or British policy in China, he says so just as plainly as if he were still a mere Senator. If he does not like what he hears about the intentions of the President in respect to the French debt, he says so loudly and publicly. He feels perfectly free to indulge in running comment on the acts of foreign powers, on the domestic affairs of other nations, on their statesmen and their national habits, on their ambitions and supposed purposes, and on any and all negotiations however delicate at any time while they are in progress. He is not concerned apparently about the difficulty which foreigners experience because they do not know whether they are being lectured by

William E. Borah of Idaho or by the Senate of the United States as a coördinate part of the treaty-making power.

He feels himself privileged to use the prestige of his office to promote the influence of his opinions. The ensuing troubles of the Executive do not break his heart, and the demands of all institutions that men suppress themselves and conform mean very little to him. Mr. Borah is a confirmed bachelor who somehow finds himself married to the Executive. I do not say he will be unfaithful, but Heaven pity the Executive if it expects Borah to worry about the whole damn family.

As a matter of fact he regards it as his high duty to watch the Executive with the utmost suspicion. The history of secret diplomacy in Europe has made a deep impression on him and he believes that the wars and miseries of mankind are due chiefly to the irresponsible intrigues of diplomats. He has also a sublime faith that legislatures and popular majorities are in the nature of things pacific and just. It is the very essence of his philosophy that bad deeds are done in the dark, and that light brings righteousness. I have never detected the quiver of a doubt on his part that this is one of the eternal verities, but also I do not recall any attempt on his part to consider the weight of popular prejudice which beats upon a statesman who might wish to appease the Japanese, or to deal rationally with debts and reparations. It is a fundamental fact about Borah that he accepts the dogma of open diplomacy at face value.

V

It will be a decisive fact in the immediate future of our foreign relations that Senator Borah looks upon the ancient prerogatives of the Senate as suited to the practice of open diplomacy. Other chairmen of the Committee, Senator Lodge for example, have been jealous to maintain the rights of the Senate against the President, but they have been moved, if I read them correctly, by the inveterate desire of all men to hold and extend a vested right. But Mr. Borah is moved by a passion to thwart evil by publicity, and the powers of the Senate are for him a means to that end. He is more determined than Mr. Lodge ever was to make the Senate a major partner in diplomatic affairs, for Mr. Borah plays no favorites and cares nothing, where Mr. Lodge cared much, for the unity and the glory of the Republican Party. Mr. Borah's insistence on the rôle of the Senate is inspired, therefore, by a faith that meant little to Mr. Lodge. It is a faith in the ultimate righteousness of an appeal to the people. If the Senators were consulted and if the Senators advised, Mr. Lodge was satisfied. He insisted that the President recognize the Senators. Mr. Borah, on the other hand, conceives it to be the duty of the Senate to force the President to consult the whole electorate.

Thus Senator Borah is engaged in trying to turn the treaty-making powers of the Senate into the means to a very open popular diplomacy. The experiment will be well worth watching because surely there can be no doubt that with the increase of contact across frontiers various interests within each nation are bound to play a larger part in the conduct of foreign policy. It has ceased to be possible for diplomacy to be in the sole keeping of the head of the state. The Executive must obtain the advice and consent of many people if his engagements with a foreign nation are to be binding. The question is whether the constitutional powers of the Senate under Article 2, Section 2, can be stretched to cover this new need.

They were not designed to make possible an open diplomacy. The authors of the Constitution certainly did not suppose that they were compelling the President to open up the whole conduct of foreign policy to popular discussion. *The Federalist* commends Article 2, Section 2, because it "provides that our negotiations for treaties shall have every advantage which can be derived from talents, information, integrity and deliberate investigation on the one hand, and from secrecy and dispatch on the other." In another place the writers of *The Federalist* argue that the House of Representatives is not fit to participate because "decision, secrecy and dispatch are incompatible with the genius of a body so variable and so numerous." It is plain that the authors of the Constitution thought that the President would consult in secret with a small body of men; there were only twenty-six Senators at that time, and the President needed only to convince about eighteen of them. The House which the Fathers rejected as too variable and too numerous was then smaller than the present Senate. It consisted of only sixty-five members. President Washington himself tried once to consult the small Senate of that day about the treaty with the Creek Indians, and had such an unpleasant time that he never tried it again. Later when the House asked him for information about the Jay Treaty he refused, saying that "the nature of foreign relations requires caution and their success must often depend on secrecy."

While it is clear enough what the authors of the Constitution meant, they did not state what they meant very clearly. The phrase, "advice and consent," was so vague that it left room for a large development of our constitutional practice. Thus by the beginning of the twentieth century the powers of the Senate had, at least in the opinion of Senator Lodge, grown to the point where the Senate virtually had the right to negotiate independently with a foreign power. The doctrine of Lodge is worth looking at here, for our hero, Mr. Borah, has adopted it and is making the fullest possible use of it.

The doctrine was enunciated by Mr. Lodge in an article written for *Scribner's Magazine* in 1902 and reprinted by the Senate in 1921. Mr. Lodge felt that a little lecture on American constitutional law was in order, for Lord Landsdowne, then Secretary of State for Foreign Affairs, had evinced a regrettable inability to understand the Senate. The noble lord said he was puzzled by the behavior of the Senate in amending the Hay-Pauncefote Treaty; he complained that contrary to well-established international usage His Majesty's Government, "without any previous attempts to ascertain their views," had suddenly been confronted with a new proposal. Lord Lansdowne was used to dealing with foreign offices, but he had never yet been asked to conduct a diplomatic negotiation with a branch of the legislature.

Mr. Lodge proceeded, icily and firmly, to set him right:

"Mr. Hay and Lord Pauncefote open a negotiation for the modification of the Clayton-Bulwer Treaty. . . . After due discussion they agree upon and sign a treaty. That agreement, so far as Great Britain is concerned, requires only the approval of the King for its completion, but with the United States it is very different, because no treaty can be ratified by the President of the United States without the consent of the Senate. . . . *But he (Lord Lansdowne) does not seem to have realized that the Senate could properly continue the negotiations begun by Mr. Hay and Lord Pauncefote by offering new or modified propositions to His Majesty's Government."* (Italics mine.)

A treaty drawn by the President in agreement with a foreign power is still "inchoate," said Mr. Lodge; it is "a mere project for a treaty." And so a foreign power which sets out to make a treaty with the United States must deal first with the State Department at one end of Pennsylvania Avenue and then with another State Department at the other end. Lord Lansdowne must have found that very strange. He had not yet learned that a diplomatic affair with the United States is like a two-volume novel in which the hero marries the heroine at the end of the first volume and divorces her triumphantly at the end of the second.

In asserting these powers of the Senate, Mr. Lodge planted himself on the meaning of the Constitution. In the interpretation of this clause it is a case of each man his own oracle, for if one thing is clear it is that the Fathers had no very prophetic idea of how they meant Article 2, Section 2, to work. Hamilton wrote a paper on the subject for *The Federalist*, and the paper is one of the least illuminating he ever wrote. But in one clause of a sentence devoted to a very different subject he speaks of obtaining "sanction in the progressive stages of a treaty." Although this does not bear out Senator

Lodge's notion that the Senate could "continue the negotiations" by itself, it does seem to say that the Senate was to advise and consent not merely on the completed treaty, but step by step in the negotiations.

VI

The moral of it all is that the Constitution itself is so ambiguous that it could be stretched to cover any workable arrangement. The real difficulty for Mr. Borah or for any one else who wishes to see the legislature play a serious part in diplomacy is that large bodies of men cannot conduct a negotiation or initiate a policy. As a general rule they can only approve or disapprove propositions presented to them. The Senate can accept or reject a treaty; it can occasionally even adopt amendments proposed by Senators; it can make reservations. The Congress can declare war; it can appropriate money or refuse to appropriate money to carry out an international obligation. Yet these powers, great as they are, control only a very small area of diplomatic action. At the most they may be sufficient to compel the President to consider whether he can enlist the support of the legislature for the policies he is pursuing. The President is like a general with a somewhat mutinous army on his hands; he cannot be sure his troops will follow him. Occasionally his troops will run away from him. But whether his troops obey or disobey they do not determine the strategy of the campaign. He determines the strategy in the light of the support he can muster.

The attempt of a legislature to control foreign policy is in the nature of things an attempt to make the tail wag the dog. Congress alone, for example, has the power to declare war. But the President has the power to make war and to put Congress in the position where it must either back him up or haul down the flag. The Executive who believes a war is necessary can create a situation where Congress really has no choice. He can occupy ports, shoot off the cannon, and get himself embroiled so that no patriotic legislature will refuse to help him out. It is something of a fiction to say that Congress alone can declare war. It is nearer the truth to say that Congress has a theoretical right to decide whether a war which has already begun shall be continued. But Congress has no power to say how long the war shall be continued; for the President can make an armistice when he chooses.

The power of the Senate over treaties is no less elusive. In theory no covenant binding the action of the United States can be made without its consent; in fact every President makes decisions which are binding without the consent of the Senate. He may do this by exchange of notes, by gentlemen's agreements, by the mere fact that when the President does one thing something else follows by the logic of necessity. The intervention of the Senate when formal treaties are presented to it occurs in the

presence of a mountain of accomplished facts. The
Senate can tinker a little with the text, but as a
general practice it must take it or leave it. And
even if the Senate takes the treaty, the real meaning
of the treaty eludes the Senate because the power of
interpretation and administration remains with the
Executive. "Whoever hath an absolute authority
to interpret any written or spoken laws," said Bishop
Hoadley, "it is he who is truly the law-giver to all
intents and purposes."

How very elusive is the legislative control of
foreign affairs may be seen by a remarkable memorandum in the Roosevelt papers.[1] On July 29, 1905,
the Japanese Premier, Count Katsura, had a "conversation" with a personal representative of President Roosevelt. This spokesman, who remains
anonymous to this day, was not a member of the
State Department. The conversation was secret,
and the agreed memorandum of it was confirmed by
a telegram from the President. It is a statement
of Roosevelt's Far Eastern policy, and contains the
following passage:

"The Count well understands the traditional
policy of the United States . . . and perceives
fully the impossibility of their entering into a formal
alliance . . . with foreign nations, but in view of
our common interests he could (not) see why some

[1] For text, *cf.* Tyler Dennett, "Roosevelt and the Russo-Japanese
War," p. 112.

good understanding, or an alliance in practice if not in name, should not be made between these three (Britain, Japan, and the United States) nations, in so far as respects affairs in the Far East. With such understanding firmly formed, general peace in these regions would be easily maintained to the great benefit of all concerned.

"(The American spokesman) said that it was difficult, indeed impossible, for the President of the United States to enter even to an understanding amounting in effect to a confidential informal agreement, without the consent of the Senate, but that he felt sure that without any agreement at all the people of the United States was so fully in accord with the people of Japan and Great Britain in the maintenance of peace in the Far East that whatever occasion arose appropriate action of the Government of the United States, in conjunction with Japan and Great Britain, for such a purpose could be counted on by them quite as confidently as if the United States were under treaty obligations to take (it)."

All this was quite correct, no doubt, for it explicitly disclaims a formal alliance. But it was none the less a secret understanding about a great international question, and the Senate was not consulted. This is not an isolated case. One could duplicate it, I believe, many times in the administrations of other Presidents because the necessity of reaching agreements with foreign powers overrides all theory.

President Roosevelt at the time wrote to George Kennan, who had proposed an open alliance with Japan and Britain, that he was "talking academically. . . . I might just as well strive for the moon as for such a policy as you indicate. Mind you, I personally entirely agree with you." And yet he gave Count Katsura fairly definite assurances, much in the spirit of a man who obeys the Volstead Act but has a refined bootlegger.

The effort of the Senate to control the conduct of foreign affairs is bound to be spasmodic, to be feeble as a general rule, but now and then powerfully obstructive. A continuous control in the present state of the world is out of the question. As long as the relations between great states remain essentially combative, until, if ever, their relations are reduced to established law and a formal, orderly, and leisurely procedure, the open, popular control of diplomacy which Mr. Borah desires will remain largely an aspiration. It is incompatible with the prevailing anarchy of heavily armed sovereign states. It is suited only to a pacific world in which there are no dangerous decisions to be made, in which any question can be debated and bungled without fatal damage in the rough and tumble of legislatures and elections. The internal peace of the United States is so profound that the methods of Congress are at the worst an inconvenience. But the peace of the world is so fragile that those same methods would convulse it in an unending agitation.

It is the fundamental paradox of Mr. Borah's
career that he combines a passion for open diplomacy
with a passionate objection to every step toward
that world organization under which open diplomacy
might ultimately become feasible. Unless he changes
more than most men of his eminence change at his
age, it is too much to expect that he will resolve
that paradox. Mr. Borah is not the kind of man
to subject himself to the labor of following through
in a patient way the implications of his own ideal.
He is a self-sufficient man with great confidence in
the promptings of his own conscience. He shrinks
instinctively from a train of thought which might
compel him to revise certain of his passionate
negations, and from a course of action which it
would be difficult to explain to large audiences. The
definite pursuit of the ideal of open diplomacy
would carry him into regions where he is not at
home, into fields of coöperation which are unsuited
to his temperament.

For he is a virtuoso who plays by ear. He is a
powerful obstructor of good and of evil, always
gallant and sometimes perverse. Amidst trimmers
and place warmers he is a gadfly to the bureaucratic
and the toplofty. He is an immense advertisement
for the idea of open diplomacy. Like the universe
and like the weather the only thing to do about
Borah is to accept him. You will find him very
useful to-morrow, and you should not complain, then,
if he leaves the confused relationship of the Presi-

dent and the Senate no less confused, and the anarchic relations of sovereign states no less anarchic. A man, even when by accident he becomes Chairman of the Committee on Foreign Relations, does not change his character.

January, 1926.

"THE OUTLAWRY OF WAR"

I

DURING the war it was generally believed that the way to prevent war in the future was to make war swiftly and unitedly on all future Germanys. Theodore Roosevelt, as early as September, 1914, had urged the formation of what he called an international *posse comitatus* against "outlaw" nations. This same suggestion was adopted subsequently, under the name of a League to Enforce Peace, by Mr. Taft, Senator Lodge, and others. In the spring of 1916 President Wilson was publicly converted to the idea that a war of aggression was the concern not merely of the attacking nation and its victim, but of all civilized nations, that an attack on one was an attack on all, that a breach of the peace should in the future be answered by united enforcement of peace. It was in this context of thought and feeling that a Chicago lawyer,

Mr. S. O. Levinson, launched his proposal for "the
outlawry of war." [1]

Political leaders had not yet divided along
partisan lines, and with two million American men
on their way to French battlefields none expressed
any dislike of European entanglements.   Mr.
Levinson was safe in assuming that what the United
States was then doing, in March, 1918, it would in
the event of another aggression do again.   Therefore, it was naturally in the current of public opinion
for Mr. Levinson to argue that the Roosevelt-Taft-
Lodge-Wilson theory of a League to Enforce
Peace would be strengthened and clarified if war
itself were declared a punishable crime in international law.   There would then be no hesitant
neutrality, no doubt about the right and duty of all
nations to join in the war against a nation like
Germany.   Mr. Levinson's phrase, therefore, seemed
less novel then than it does now.   For in the mood
of those days he had merely found a rather pictur-
esque name for the generally accepted theory of a
war against war.

The same idea was, of course, taken to Paris by
President Wilson.   But of Mr. Levinson's phrase
nothing much was heard until a year afterward when
the first draft of the Covenant of the League of
Nations was printed.   Then the phrase reappeared

---

[1] S. O. LEVINSON: "The Legal Status of War," in *The New Republic,* March 9, 1918; *cf.* also JOHN DEWEY: "Morals and the Conduct
of Status," in *The New Republic,* March 23, 1918.

in a speech delivered by the late Senator Philander C. Knox. But there had begun a radical change of meaning. The phrase which Mr. Levinson had coined to clarify the purposes of a League to Enforce Peace was now the name of a substitute for the League of Nations. For Mr. Knox, who was the acknowledged leader of the irreconcilables in the Senate, their most courageous guide and their shrewdest counselor, was not content with a purely destructive attack on President Wilson's project. He acknowledged the need of a substitute, and he started out with Mr. Levinson's help to construct a new plan for peace.

In Senator Knox's first speech, delivered the first of March, 1919, the "outlawry of war" is still associated with the idea of a League to Enforce Peace. Mr. Knox is definitely opposed to the League of Nations, but he continues to discuss "a league," based upon a "constitution" which is to call upon "the powers signatory to enforce" the decrees and awards of an international court, "as against unwilling states, by force, economic pressure, or otherwise." However, within a few months, concurrently with the rising tide of American opinion against the League and all covenants to use force, Mr. Knox and Mr. Levinson changed their minds. In formulating their "plan to outlaw war," they cast aside not only *the* League, but *a* league as well, and deprived their international court of any power to enforce its decrees.

After the death of Senator Knox the outlawry of war seemed for a time to be forgotten. President Harding alluded to it at the opening of the Washington Conference, but nothing was done with his suggestion. Then early in 1923 Senator Borah adopted the slogan and the idea, and became the political leader of what is now an organized campaign. Mr. Borah is advocating the "outlawry of war" and the defeat of the Permanent Court of International Justice.

We find then that the phrase was first employed in order to strengthen a league before there was a League. It was used to defeat the League after there was a League, and to advocate an international court before there was a Court. Now that the Court has been created, it is being used to defeat the Court, and to advocate another court which does not exist.

II

The phrase is associated, then, as a matter of political history, with a perfect record of irreconcilability. But this association is, I think, personal and accidental. It was a chance happening that Senator Knox adopted the phrase in his attack on the League. It is a chance happening that Senator Borah uses the phrase in his attack on the Court. For there are many devoted adherents to the League, beginning with Lord Robert Cecil, who would like to find a way to define war and outlaw it. There are many

who support the existing Court, beginning with Mr.
Elihu Root, who also would like to outlaw war. The
phrase is as appropriate in Lord Robert Cecil's
mouth as it was in Mr. Knox's, in Mr. Root's as in
Mr. Borah's. It is only an accident of irreconcilable
politics in the United States Senate which has identified "the outlawry of war" with active opposition
to every established institution for the prevention of
war.

How accidental is this association may be judged
from the position of Senator Borah. Not once, but
many times, Mr. Borah is on record against the
League because it is alleged to be a superstate which
will destroy our national sovereignty. But this belief
about the League does not deter Mr. Borah from
employing his eloquence to deride the existing World
Court because it has no power to take jurisdiction
in all international disputes! Because there has not
been formulated by world conference an authoritative code of law covering the matters about which
nations dispute! Mr. Borah's confirmed objections
to a superstate sleep comfortably in the same mind
with his demand for a Supreme Court of the World,
modeled on our Federal Supreme Court, having its
gigantic powers in conflicts between states, including,
if Mr. Borah's analogy means anything, the power
to annul acts of parliaments, including acts of our
own Congress!

A position so illogical must be a political accident.

There can be no necessary connection between the outlawry of war and the orthodox philosophy of the irreconcilables. There is, rather, a deep contradiction between them, a contradiction so deep that it has produced the extraordinary spectacle of Mr. Borah objecting to a superstate and at the same time demanding a supercourt, and a superconference to legislate a supercode. We have nevertheless to discuss the outlawry of war in this setting, as a project for world peace offered by the irreconcilable opponents of the existing League and the existing Court. With proposals to work for the outlawry of war through existing international organizations, such as Lord Robert Cecil and Mr. Root have entertained, we are not here concerned. We are faced with the fact that the American campaign for the outlawry of war is led by men who have fought and will continue to fight not only the League and the Court, but even such conventions as were reached at the Washington Conference.

Narrow is the path and straight is the gate for those who wish to join Mr. Borah's campaign for the outlawry of war. The idea of attempting to make war a crime still belongs to men of all shades of opinion. But the "outlawry of war," as a political label, is now the name of what purports to be a comprehensive plan of world peace, fundamentally different from any yet attempted, and in the test of action, antagonistic to all.

III

The Borah plan for abolishing war is embodied in Senate Resolution 441, introduced on February 14, 1923. The plan has three parts: first there is to be a universal treaty making war "a public crime under the law of nations" and "a solemn agreement or treaty to bind" every nation "to indict and punish its own international war breeders or instigators and war profiteers";

Second, there is to be "created and adopted . . . a code of international law of peace based upon equality and justice between nations, amplified and expanded and adapted and brought down to date";

Third, there is to be created "a judicial substitute for war" or (if existing, in part adapted and adjusted) in the form or nature of an international court, modeled on our Federal Supreme Court in its jurisdiction over controversies between our sovereign states, such court to possess affirmative jurisdiction to hear and decide all purely international controversies as defined by the code, or arising under treaties."

This is the scheme which in Mr. Borah's opinion is to abolish war. This is the scheme which is to do what the League and Court, in his opinion, cannot do. This is the scheme which has such promise of effectiveness, in the minds of the advocates of the outlawry of war, that they are determined to defeat not only American adherence to the League, but the modest proposal of President Harding to adhere to the Court. It is this scheme, they say, or none. There is no other way to end war.

What they are relying upon fundamentally is not their court and their code, but the treaty "outlawing war." They believe that this slogan has the power to arouse and then to crystallize mankind's abhorrence of war. They believe a declaration that war is a crime would legalize pacifism throughout the world, and deprive the war spirit of its legality and authority. The war-maker would then have to be the conscientious objector, the pacifist would be under the shelter of law and order and conservatism. Once this radical reversal of patriotic and legal values had taken place, war would be almost unorganizable, because pacifism would be the authoritative morality of the nations.

We are dealing then primarily with a moral crusade in favor of complete moral disarmament. If the propaganda were successful, machinery for keeping the peace would not be very necessary, because the propaganda itself, so its sponsors argue, would destroy the will to war. Once nations had learned not to wish to fight, keeping the peace would be an easy matter. Therefore, the advocates of the plan, except for controversial purposes, have given little thought to, and place little emphasis upon, their project for a new court and a new code.

Nevertheless, before men commit themselves universally to a pacifism so radical that it destroys the

patriotic code which they are accustomed to associate
with their security and their national destiny, it is
likely that they will inquire very closely into Mr.
Borah's machinery for keeping the peace. He will
have to prove, I think, that his court and his code
effectively promise to prevent war, if he is to induce
mankind to disarm, first morally and then physically.
Men will scrutinize rather closely this new code and
this new court under which, having rendered themselves militarily impotent, they are to live.

IV

It is clearly easier to arouse large audiences to
a denunciation of war in general than it is to persuade them to agree on the principles of a code.
Men agree that war is a horror and a crime. They
do not agree easily on the fixing of boundaries, the
right to secede, the right of revolution, the control
of raw materials, access to the sea, the rights of
minorities, tariffs, immigration, the status of colonies, the rights of property. They do not agree
easily about what constitute, in Mr. Borah's words,
"purely international controversies." People are
fairly unanimous against war. They are wholly
unanimous in their professions of love for "equality
and justice." But they quarrel fearfully about what
is just and what is equal. They are divided over
the general principles which ought to decide great
issues. They are even more divided over the inter-

pretation of the facts in specific cases under general principles.

Shall boundaries be determined by nationality or by economic geography? May Ireland secede from the Empire, may Ulster secede from Ireland, may three counties secede from Ulster? Is revolution permitted? Is revolution assisted by a foreign power permitted? Are the natural resources of undeveloped countries the property of the natives to have and to hold as they see fit, or have European and American nations rights in them, and how are those rights to be apportioned? Do nations which happen to block the access of other nations to the sea owe any duty to landlocked peoples, which ought to limit their sovereign rights over their own ports and railroads? Are national and religious minorities, whether they be Germans in Poland or Negroes in Mississippi, to be protected by any rule of international law? Is the tariff a "purely" domestic question? Is prohibition "applied to foreign ships" a domestic question? Is discrimination against immigrants a domestic question? Have colonies the right to revolt? May Mexico confiscate American oil property? May the United States confiscate sealed liquor on foreign ships?

Now when Senator Borah proposes to create a code of international law as a substitute for war he must mean, if he means anything, a code which establishes legal rules covering such questions. But who is to make such a code? Mr. Borah's resolution does not tell us. The Knox-Levinson plan calls for a world conference to perform the feat, and other advocates speak of a convention of experts and jurists. Little attempt is ever made to describe how this code is to be made. The point is passed over lightly with some reference to the codification and creation of international law.

But the word "creation" is perhaps the biggest word in the English language. To create a code "based on equality and justice" is to legislate authoritatively on all the major classes of disputes in which nations engage. Nothing like it is attempted under the existing League. For his plan involves, whether Mr. Borah likes the name or not, the setting-up of a world legislature. The conference which was to make the code would have to lay down laws affecting the very existence of governments and the destiny of nations. It would have to legislate on questions touching their political independence, their liberties, their power, their prestige, their economic opportunities, and their pride.

To talk easily about a conference to create an international code is either idle talk, or it is as stupendous a proposal as can be conceived in politics. It requires for the first time in human history the creation of a genuine world legislature. For, if the code was to be anything more than a set of pious evasions, no one world conference could conceivably create it. One might as well have expected the first United States Congress to create in its first session a code of American national law. No: this world conference would have to convene and reconvene, and keep on, in the words of Mr. Borah's resolution, amplifying the code, and expanding it, and adapting it, and bringing it down to date.

This world legislature would unavoidably represent the cabinets and foreign offices of the day. Can any one imagine a government which did not keep a death grip on a delegation which was legislating on a rule affecting, let us say, the national boundaries? And thus there vanishes wholly the hope that the world can be governed, to use Mr. John Dewey's terms, by "legal coöperation" without "political combination." If there is to be law for the court to apply, there must be lawmakers. And lawmakers are politicians, guided for the most part by the pressures of their constituents upon their own ambitions and habits and personal ideals. Let Mr. Borah ask himself, then, whether he is prepared to entrust the creation of such a code to Lord Curzon, Mr. Hughes, M. Poincaré, and Baron Kato, or to any other men he knows. And then let him ask himself whether he thinks the United States Senate will ratify a code that all the other parliaments of the world will also ratify.

It requires no gift of prophecy to see that if he could induce the world to establish such a code, Mr. Borah and his most devoted followers would be lined up against ratification as irreconcilable opponents. They would hate the result if and when they achieved it. For any code created within this generation would have to legalize the status quo at the time the code was formulated. It is unthinkable that Great Britain, France, Japan, or the United States would agree on any specific set of principles which impaired their empires, their Monroe Doctrines, or their alleged strategic requirements. Lest there be any doubt on this point I quote from Senator Knox's original speech of March 1, 1919, proposing the outlawry of war: "Under such a code we would not be called upon to arbitrate the policy involved in our Monroe Doctrine, our conservation policy, our immigration policy, our right to expel aliens, our right to repel invasion, our right to maintain military and naval establishments, or coaling-stations, within our borders or elsewhere as the protection and development of this country might demand, our right to make necessary fortifications of the Panama Canal or on our frontiers, our right to discriminate between natives and foreigners in respect to right of property and citizenship, and other matters of like character."

We must not be called upon, said Senator Knox, to arbitrate these questions. In other words, we would go to war rather than yield our position.

One may call this the outlawry of war if one likes, but I suspect that a foreigner would call it the outlawry of those wars which might interfere with Senator Knox's conception of the interests, needs, and manifest destiny of the United States. Let fifty other nations also draw up a catalogue of questions over which they would rather fight than submit to a tribunal, and the amount of war you will have outlawed will not be noticeable.

V

The advocates of this plan are fond of saying that the "war system," consisting of armaments, alliances, and the diplomacy of prestige and strategic advantages, rests upon the fact that war is "legalized." Whether this be a correct analysis is not important in view of the fact that the advocates of the outlawry of war propose to continue to legalize all kinds of wars. "War shall be defined in the code," says the Knox-Levinson plan, "and the right of defense against actual or imminent attack shall be preserved." Senator Borah's resolution seems to justify, in addition, wars of liberation. Now if you have the right to go to war for what you call your liberty, and the right to go to war because you think an attack is imminent, it would be a stupid Foreign Office indeed which could not legalize any war it thought necessary or desirable. The only war outlawed under this plan is a war openly announced to be a war of aggression. There are no such wars.

The wars permitted under the outlawry of war are not confined to the defense of frontiers against invasion. If that were the case the advocates of the plan would agree to submit every international dispute to an international tribunal. We have seen that Senator Knox has no idea of doing any such thing. His list of disputes that may not be arbitrated covered all the really vital disputes in which the United States is likely to be involved. It covered all the main contentions with Japan, the whole field of Latin-American relations, our whole economic policy, our whole strategic and military system, and for good measure everything that "the protection and development of the country might demand." Senator Borah, though less specific, is no less definitely against arbitrating vital questions. His way of excluding them from judicial processes is to deny that they are "purely international controversies." But of course controversies between nations are none the less controversies because you choose not to call them international controversies. If you feel I am hurting you badly, you are not pacified by my telling you to mind your own business.

The Borah plan to outlaw war consists of a code which, in theory, outlaws war and lays down rules governing all the relations among governments. But it consists also of a set of reservations which withdraw from the scope of the code and the competence of the court many, if not most, of the major policies which cause disputes. Finally it disembowels the outlawry of war by legalizing wars in defense of those major policies which are excluded from the competence of the court and the code.

Mr. Borah, in other words, is proposing to outlaw

those wars which can be described as "purely international." He is proposing to outlaw theoretical wars which nobody wishes to wage, since all actual wars result out of the conflict of sovereign, domestic interests. A "purely international controversy" which does not involve, or appear to involve, the domestic safety, domestic interests, or the domestic pride of the disputants is not worth worrying about. Even in this wicked and pugnacious world such a harmless and uninteresting controversy does not often lead to war. To outlaw war simply in respect to such controversies is a lot of trouble for nothing. For, until a man is willing to say that he is ready to submit any and every dispute affecting the peace of the world to adjudication, he has not made up his mind to outlaw war. An irreconcilable senator, who is jealous of American sovereignty, can play with the idea. He cannot really understand it and still believe in it.

VI

It is illuminating to inquire how an idea like the outlawry of war, which expresses so deep an aspiration, should have become so confused and sterile. The answer is to be found, I think, in Mr. Borah's resolution, where he says that "the genius of civilization has discovered but two methods of compelling the settlement of human disputes; namely, law and war." Mr. Borah means by law the judicial process, and in my opinion his generalization is utterly untrue.

The genius of civilization has invented, besides law and war, countless other methods of settling disputes. It has invented diplomacy, representative government, federalism, mediation, conciliation, friendly intervention, compromise, and conference. The notion that the judicial process in a court is the only method of peace is fantastic. Mr. Borah, every day of his life, is engaged in adjusting disputes between the state of Idaho and other states, between capital and labor, between the farm bloc and the manufacturers and bankers. If he believed that the only alternative to war was resort to the courts, he would not be wasting his talents in a nonjudicial body like the United States Senate. He would either be a judge or be arguing before judges.

Nevertheless he believes, and many admirable people believe with him, that the only method of international peace is "to create a judicial substitute for war." It is on this belief that the outlawry of war has foundered. For when you come to the actual task of creating this judicial substitute, you find, as Mr. Knox found and as Mr. Borah has found, that you cannot, or will not, devise a code of international law covering all disputes, and that you will not give to any court jurisdiction over all disputes. Therefore, in the pinch, you find yourself wishing to outlaw war but not to outlaw the wars you may feel compelled to wage.

You find a large class of disputes which your judicial substitute will not cover. They are the most important disputes of all, because they involve precisely those vital interests about which people are most ready to fight. The difficulty is fundamental and inescapable in any plan to outlaw war by a purely judicial substitute. And, if you are really in earnest about minimizing or abolishing war, it is these marginal, nonjusticiable disputes which must occupy the center of attention.

By the growth of international law some of these disputes can be made justiciable. But, for as long a future as we can foresee, there will remain whole classes of the most dangerous disputes which no code and no court can deal with. For them diplomacy is required, diplomacy working by conference, compromise, bargaining, good offices, and also, in the last analysis, I believe, by the threat of force. One may admit the rôle of force in diplomacy without embarrassment, considering how thoroughly the right to wage war is actually reserved by the advocates of the outlawry of war.

The central fallacy of their argument is this refusal to acknowledge the necessity of diplomacy for just those war-breeding disputes which are not within the competence of their code and their court. For, if diplomacy is a necessary method of maintaining peace, then no plan which does not provide for it can be an effective plan to abolish war. And if the method of diplomacy is necessary, then the reform of that method is one of the most urgent of human needs.

For "the diplomatic method," as Mr. Root has pointed out, "is the necessary method of dealing with immediate exigencies and dangerous crises in affairs. Under such circumstances there is no other way to prevent disaster. Argument and persuasion and explanation, the removal of misapprehensions, the suggestion of obstacles and advantages, conciliation, concession, stipulations for the future, and the still more serious considerations to which diplomacy may finally resort—all these are employed to deal with immediate and acute situations. The slow processes of judicial procedure are not adapted to deal with such exigencies."

Mr. Root might have added that the judicial procedure inevitably is corrupted if it is burdened with the making of major political decisions. For, if the judges of Mr. Borah's Court are asked to decide questions for which no rule of law exists, they must either invent a law and thus legislate, or, in the guise of law, they must make political deals. Mr. Borah, therefore, is not eliminating political entanglements. He is entangling his proposed court in the politics of the world. The result would be a court with all the vices of politics and a diplomacy as cumbersome as a lawsuit.

This conclusion may be tested by considering another remarkable statement in Mr. Borah's resolution. It is a pronouncement to the effect that our Supreme Court has maintained peace between the states. If that is true, what has been the function of

the Executive and the Congress these last one
hundred and thirty-five years? Does Senator Borah
seriously think our Supreme Court, existing in a
political vacuum, could have adjusted the sectional,
group, and class conflicts of American history? He
cannot think that, and therefore, when he has
stopped to consider the matter, he cannot continue
to think that an international court, in vacuo, can
maintain the peace of the world.

But Mr. Borah has not fully considered the matter. He speaks in his resolution of conferring upon
a "real" international court jurisdiction modeled
upon that of our Supreme Court. Mr. Borah has no
smallest intention of doing any such thing. We may
dogmatically assert this because we shall as soon behold the sun stand still in the sky as see the irreconcilable Senator from Idaho argue that nine judges
at the Hague should have the same power to annul
a law passed by Parliament or Congress as our
Supreme Court has to annul the acts of a state
legislature.

VII

Mr. Borah is not really promoting a practicable
project that will stand up under analysis. He is
giving currency to a metaphor, and a somewhat inaccurate metaphor at that, which, like its predecessor, "the war to end war," condenses and expresses,
but does not direct toward any organized result,
the hatred of war. Incidentally, though that is no

part of this discussion, he is exploiting the sentiment which the metaphor evokes in order to prevent our adherence to the only world court which exists, or in this generation is likely to exist. Once more we witness the tragic futility of noble sentiments frustrated by confused ideas.

Once more a fine aspiration, which must be universal in order to prevail, has become entangled in the prejudices and politics of a faction. Once more we behold the spectacle, so delightful to Satan, of men who wish to establish universal confidence and coöperation on earth, refusing in the smallest measure to coöperate among themselves. It is a pity. For if Mr. Borah and his friends took the ideal of world coöperation seriously, and understood its difficulties, they would count it no slight matter that fifty sovereign nations have actually agreed on something, even though that something is as defective as the existing League and the existing Court. If Mr. Borah loved his ideal of coöperation as constantly as he yields to his habit of irreconcilability, he would wish to promote, rather than to destroy, what coöperation there is. For only by practice can coöperation become a habit. And only when coöperation is a powerful habit, will peoples be willing to make the enormous sacrifices which the outlawry of war must finally involve. But to say to the world, as Mr. Borah's associates have in effect done from the start, that mankind must meet our terms or none, and coöperate on our principles or none, is to perpetuate precisely that temper of mind which the outlawry of war will most need to outlaw.

Nor can we say to mankind: "Under the leadership of an American President we led you into a League of Nations, and under the intellectual leadership of an American lawyer we led you, with the apparent blessing of both political parties, into the Permanent Court of International Justice. Now that you are in, and we are outside, it occurs to us to lead you out of the League and out of the Court. When you are out of the League and out of the Court we led you into, we promise to lead you into a much better court and perhaps even into another association of nations."

Were the Senate now to reject the existing Court, we should establish our reputation as a diplomatic philanderer. Prudent foreign governments when we made our next periodic proposal would have to ask bluntly whether the young man's intentions were serious and honorable.

August, 1923.

THE GREATNESS OF MR. MELLON

I

IT is often a puzzle to know just how a popular idea goes into circulation. There is, for example, the idea that Andrew W. Mellon is a very great Secretary of the Treasury. Where did that idea come from? Not, I venture to suggest, from any close popular appreciation of the conduct of the Treasury, for the work of the Treasury is for the most part too technical to be appreciated by more than a few members of Congress and a small circle of financial experts. The man in the smoking car who says Mr. Mellon is the greatest Secretary since Alexander Hamilton would find it hard to describe either the greatness of Alexander Hamilton or the greatness of Andrew W. Mellon. The idea of greatness has been put into such extensive circulation, however, that it has now become one of the sacred cows of American public thinking.

Once you have seen Mr. Mellon it is easy to think of him as a great man. He has a kind of lean elegance which distinguishes him at once in any large gathering of officials. There is none of that bleary and pudgy look which public men take on by eating too much and smoking too much and listening too much and talking too much. He has the air of quiet command; a dignity and reserve which make him seem remote, like the portrait of an ancestor, from the contemporary scene. But since he is the maker and owner of one of the largest private fortunes ever known, his competence in this world does not have to be proved by the usual sonorous cajolery.

I do not pretend to know very much about all the men who have been Secretary of the Treasury, or even to know anything about most of them. Perhaps there are a few others who are equally ignorant. But I have read a good many books about Hamilton, and I can see why Mr. Mellon can justly be compared with Hamilton, although the comparison is very unflattering to Mr. Mellon. Both men believe that the salvation of the country was in government by the rich, especially by rich manufacturers and creditors. Between the times of Hamilton and of Mr. Mellon this philosophy was often practiced, but it was rarely avowed. For the century and more which separates the two Secretaries public discussion in this country was Jeffersonian in tone. It was the farmer, the debtor, the consumer who was appealed to and flattered. But with the advent of Andrew W. Mellon the premises of Hamilton were revived. The Republican Party ceased to hide its rich men under a bushel; it frankly asserted its belief in them once more as the rulers of the country.

Here to my mind the similarity between Hamilton and Mr. Mellon ends, and the radical difference begins. The difference is that Hamilton believed in plutocracy as the means to an end; Mr. Mellon believes in plutocracy as an end in itself. Hamilton turned toward the plutocracy because he knew it was then the strongest possible foundation on which to construct an independent and stable government. He used the rich for a purpose that was greater than their riches. But Mr. Mellon, so far as one can ascertain his ideas, is not building up the plutocracy for any purpose that transcends the accumulation of wealth.

It may be said that prosperity is a good purpose, and that Mr. Mellon believes that by encouraging the rich he is helping to maintain prosperity. I am not denying that prosperity is pleasant and desirable.

But if Hamilton were alive today, facing the problems that come to Mr. Mellon for solution, I am inclined to think that he would not rest content with prosperity as an end in itself.

Both Hamilton and Mr. Mellon have had to deal with the funding of great debts. In Hamilton's time the debt was owed by the poorer Americans to the richer Americans. In Mr. Mellon's time the debt is owed by foreign countries which are comparatively poor to this country which is comparatively rich. Both Secretaries insisted that the debt be paid. Hamilton insisted because the way to establish the credit of the Federal Government was to unite the fortunes of the moneyed classes with the fortunes of the young Republic. What purpose has Mr. Mellon had in mind in his debt-funding operations? What is he trying to do that is comparable with the purposes of Hamilton? In the answer to that question lies, I think, the test of whether Mr. Mellon is even remotely a great Secretary of the Treasury.

I say this because the funding of the international debts is by every consideration the most critical affair with which Mr. Mellon has had to deal. Nothing else in his Administration of the Treasury is of more than passing importance. I am told that he has dealt skilfully with the domestic floating debt of the United States and has taken good advantage of the money market. That is excellent, but any first-rate banker could have done it. Mr. Mellon advocated a reduction of taxes. That is popular and most welcome to those of us who pay an income tax. But nobody, I suppose, would argue that it is greatness in a Secretary of the Treasury to reduce taxes when there is a surplus of money in the bank. Mr. Mellon's plan was worked out by his two Democratic predecessors at the Treasury. Mr. Mellon has also had some odd jobs like Prohibition Enforcement. If he had handled that job well it would not make him a great Secretary of the Treasury, although it would make him a very great man. As a matter of fact Prohibition Enforcement under Mr. Mellon's titular leadership has been just what everybody knows it is: a dismal failure surrounded by foolish promises that nobody any longer believes.

The test of Mr. Mellon's greatness as a Secretary of the Treasury must certainly lie in his policy on the international debts. The consequences of that policy touch every great power in the western world. Theoretically that policy will remain for sixty-two years a considerable factor in the domestic budget and taxation of every great power in Europe, and a considerable, if not a dominating, factor in the relations between the Old World and the New. Whatever any one may think about the wisdom of the present arrangements, no one can question their importance.

Mr. Mellon has at times suggested that he was acting as the "trustee" for the American creditors of Europe. If this means that he considers himself a collecting agent, and that the international consequences are no concern of his, then all one can say is: What price greatness? What price statesmanship? If it is true that Mr. Mellon is not the author of the debt policy, if he was only carrying out what Congress and the country in its present state of mind wanted, if he does not regard this policy as the wisest policy for the long future, then there is no use of talking about him in the same breath with Alexander Hamilton. If the policy of debt collection is not Mr. Mellon's policy by conviction, if he is not responsible for it, then he is not even associated vitally with the one decisive event of his administration. Imagine Hamilton explaining away responsibility for his debt policy! Imagine Hamilton evading the unpopularity which his own conception of a sound policy involved!

Mr. Mellon has never yet made it clear whether he is convinced that the debt policy is wise. Whoever writes about Mr. Mellon must therefore choose one of two theories. Either he must say that Mr. Mellon had to bow to the will of Congress, and then he must dismiss all claims to statesmanship; or he must say that in essentials at least the debt policy is Mr. Mellon's, and in that case the political sagacity of Mr. Mellon can be measured by the quality of the debt settlements. I shall choose the second alternative as the more flattering of the two, and assume that the debt policy represents Mr. Mellon's honest conviction.

II

Let us look at this policy. Mr. Mellon has obtained agreements that the United States Government shall collect 22 billion dollars. He has proposed that the United States collect it from the four strongest nations in Europe, as well as from several smaller ones. He has proposed that the business of collecting this sum shall go on year after year, and shall end only fifteen years before the beginning of the twenty-first century.

About fifteen Presidents of the United States one after the other are to take part in this collection of money. Sixty-two British Parliaments, sixty-two French Chambers of Deputies, sixty-two Italian Parliaments, sixty-two Reichstags are to vote taxes to raise this money. Before it is all paid boys who were twenty years old when the war started will be over ninety years old. Their children, if they were born say a year after the Armistice, will be men seventy years of age. Their grandchildren will be nearly forty-five years old. Their great grandchildren will be about ready to vote. The last payment will be made in part by the great great grandchildren of the men who ruled Europe and America when the war began. They will be paying for a war as far away from them as the Civil War is from us to-day.

The sum Mr. Mellon is proposing to collect during the remainder of the century is no insignificant burden on the debtor countries. Mr. Snowden, a former Chancellor of the Exchequer, has stated that the sum paid by Britain to America costs "1,500,000 hours of labour by British workmen every day."

It is well understood that great payments from one nation to another can be made ultimately only in goods. The policy of Mr. Mellon is therefore a demand that ultimately the European debtors shall import into the United States goods valued at 22 billion dollars. Having made this demand, one would suppose that Mr. Mellon would try to find a way of getting those billions of dollars of goods out of Europe and into the United States. Nothing is further from his mind. He is a Pittsburgh manufacturer. He is a Pennsylvania Republican. He is a high protectionist by birth, by principle, and for business. He stands valiantly by his party in demanding all this wealth from Europe, and valiantly by his party's tariff in his determination to keep out all the foreign goods he can.

Now when one sits down and looks coldly at this policy, at the sums involved, at the time it is to take to collect them, at the desire both to be paid and not to be paid, it seems perfectly fantastic. So far as I know no government has ever in modern times attempted to collect money from another government for over sixty years. There have been some harsh indemnities imposed by conquerors on the conquered, but none so interminable as this one.

Never, I think, has one nation attempted to collect from all the great powers of a continent. And never has one nation charged its associates a sum comparable with this one for goods furnished in a common war. Mr. Mellon's policy is unique in history. It is something brand new. It is something nobody ever attempted before.

Yet the United States is not the first nation that loaned a great deal of money to its allies during a war. Other nations have contributed money. Other nations must, like ourselves, have wished they had the money back. But nobody until the era of Mr. Mellon has set himself grimly to such a task of debt collecting. This may be greatness. It may be originality. And then again it may be ignorance of historic experience, and a certain failure to appreciate the ways of the world.

One thing certainly Mr. Mellon has utterly failed to appreciate. That is the nature of these debts, and the necessity of convincing the debtors not only that they must be paid but that they ought to be paid. Mr. Coolidge is said to have summed up his wisdom on the subject by stating that "they hired the money, didn't they?" Mr. Mellon, or somebody speaking for him, has said repeatedly that the debts must be paid to vindicate the sanctity of contracts. Well, how much of a contract were they? The European Allies signed the notes. There is no doubt about that. But what did we give them for the notes? Did we give them money? We did not.

We gave them the right to buy guns, shells, uniforms, food, tobacco, and other necessities of war
from American manufacturers and American farmers at war prices. A part of the money paid for
these munitions the United States Treasury has long
since recovered through excess profit and income
taxes. The goods themselves were shipped to
Europe. They were used to keep the civilian population alive while the American army was being
prepared to fight. They were used to clothe and
arm and feed French and British soldiers while the
Americans were training behind the lines. They
were used immediately after the Armistice to keep
our victory from degenerating into chaos, despair,
and riot.

The theory on which Mr. Mellon has proceeded
means this: if a gun was made in the United States
and carried by a Frenchman, that gun must be paid
for with interest. But if the same kind of gun was
carried by a doughboy, we pay for it ourselves. If
we armed Frenchmen to hold the line while the
Americans were drilling in camp, the grandsons of
the Frenchmen must pay in addition to the lives
lost and the wounds suffered the price plus interest
on their guns. But when the Americans were ready
to carry the guns themselves, and to be shot themselves, it was not necessary to pay us. Now it
seems to me evident that it cost us less in every way
to have a Frenchman carry the gun through 1917.
I cannot see, and I am sure no Frenchman will

ever see, why he should pay for that gun with interest.

This practice adopted during the war of charging Frenchmen for guns they used and Americans for guns they used was a bookkeeping device. It is only lately that the distinction has become so important that it is made the foundation of an international policy which has brought us the ill will of most of the civilized world. In 1918 when people were rejoicing that at last unity of command had been achieved, Mr. Mellon would probably have been arrested as a pro-German if he had suggested to Marshal Foch that shells shot off by Frenchmen would cost France more than shells shot off by Americans. It would have been a pretty scene: Mr. Mellon arriving at G. H. Q. looking very elegant, and saying: "My dear Marshal, please remember . . . if you get those uniforms all torn and muddy you'll have nothing to show for the money you borrowed." And Marshal Foch replying: "Thank you, my dear Mr. Mellon, for reminding me. I'll send an extra division of Americans into the line. It will be cheaper for France."

III

When I consider that this is the kind of policy Mr. Mellon has made his own on the biggest question of his administration, I do not detect any trace of greatness. A great secretary, with Mr. Mellon's philosophy that the rightful rulers of this country are its big business men, would, I think, have acted quite differently. He would have seen that in the long run American business must expand all over the world or burst, and he would have used these debts, as Hamilton used the debts he funded, as bonds of tranquillity instead of as wedges of disunion throughout the world. Handled skilfully and imaginatively these debts could have been used to liquidate rapidly all the reparations and occupations and other inheritances from the war, and to set business going hopefully in Europe; handled with foresight they could have been used to further that policy of the Open Door for which Mr. Mellon's predecessors had always contended; handled with tact and sympathy they could have been used to create a fund of good will for America, worth more in cash and more in human happiness than these billions of phantom dollars.

Let no one say it could not have been done. Great Britain, too, is a creditor of the Continent, and Great Britain, with a finesse and a diplomatic insight that put our blunderers to shame, has shown how it might have been done. But only a Secretary of the Treasury with a touch of greatness could have done it, and Mr. Mellon is only a Pittsburgh millionaire.

December, 1926.

THE KELLOGG DOCTRINE: VESTED RIGHTS AND NATIONALISM IN LATIN-AMERICA

I

THE advance of American business interests into Central and South America has now reached a point where it may soon become necessary to formulate a policy as momentous as the Monroe Doctrine itself. This new policy is now in the making. The problem which it is meant to solve is the conflict between the vested rights of Americans in the natural resources of the Caribbean countries and the rising nationalism of their peoples. The problem could not have arisen before Americans had acquired titles to important properties and had invested large sums of money in developing them; nor could the problem have arisen while government of these countries was in the hands of a ruling class which conceived its interests to be those of the foreign owners of natural resources. The establishment of large American interests at a time when nationalist feeling has begun to run high has created the situation which now perplexes us in Mexico and may perplex us to-morrow in Venezuela, Colombia and elsewhere.

This is not a simple problem. We have become exporters of capital, and we are called upon to decide what is to be the attitude of the United States Government toward that exported capital when a foreign government subjects the property of American citizens to new and drastic social regulation.

II

Until quite recently the clear and dominating purpose of American policy has been to find national security. The declaration of President Monroe in his message of December 2, 1823, was a development of the original rule laid down by Washington that "in extending our commercial relations (with foreign nations) we have with them as little political connection as possible." When in May, 1823, France, acting under a commission from the Congress of Verona, put Ferdinand back upon the throne of Spain, and when Russia at the same time was advancing from Alaska down the western coast of this continent, the United States was threatened on two sides by an entanglement with the Europe of Metternich. It was threatened with a Russian Empire extending down to what is now California, and with a war to the south for the reconquest of the revolted Spanish colonies. These two threats, had they been successful, would have encircled the United States with the forces of the Quadruple Alliance, and would almost certainly have embroiled it in the dynastic politics of Europe.

Fortunately the interests of Britain, as Canning conceived them, coincided with those of the United States, and President Monroe was therefore able to state the epoch-making doctrine that bears his name. In this, its original form, the United States declared that it would resist future colonization (of European powers) in this hemisphere, and that it would "consider any attempt on their part to extend their system (*i.e.* the system of Metternich, popularly known as the Holy Alliance) to any portion of this hemisphere as dangerous to our peace and safety." This is the policy which the United States maintained with some difficulty, but in the end triumphantly, from Monroe to Roosevelt. Its purpose was American security; its method was to prevent European political intervention in this hemisphere.

The important events in the history of the Monroe Doctrine between 1823 and the beginning of this century were inspired by a determination to resist European expansion. So Clay protested in 1823 against the sale of Cuba to France, and the French withdrew their fleet. In 1843 the United States protested against the British naval occupation of

Hawaii. In 1848 Polk warned Spain and Britain against listening to the appeal of the white population of Yucatan, then engaged in a war with the Indians. Seward in 1861 protested to Spain against the occupation of Santo Domingo. And in spite of the extreme difficulties of the situation, Lincoln never recognized Maximilian in Mexico and continued to recognize Juarez. In 1895 Cleveland actually threatened war against Great Britain if the disputed boundary between Venezuela and British Guiana were not submitted to arbitration. The last and latest phase in what might be called the evolution of the simple Monroe Doctrine was the Lodge Resolution of 1912 arising out of the Magdalena Bay incident.

I have called this line of policy the simple Monroe Doctrine because it was confined to resistance to the acquisition of new territory. Thus for many years after 1823 the United States did not oppose European naval blockades of the Latin republics provided the acquisition of new territory was disclaimed. In 1825 Clay told Argentina and Brazil that they would not be protected from an "obligation the performance of which foreign nations have a right to demand." The United States did not attempt to interfere with British blockades of Nicaragua in 1842 and 1844, of Buenos Ayres in 1845, of Salvador in 1851, nor with the Spanish bombardment of Valparaiso and Callao in 1866. But when in 1902 Britain, Italy, and Germany blockaded Venezuela as a result of certain property claims, President Roosevelt became active and insistent, and according to his account had actually ordered Admiral Dewey to assemble the battle fleet at Porto Rico if the Germans did not withdraw their squadron within a certain number of days.

This was a new phase, not so much in the principle as in the practice of the American policy, and out of this incident emerged the Roosevelt corollary to the Monroe Doctrine. Two years elapsed, however, before President Roosevelt actually announced the new doctrine. Then, in connection with the occupation of Santo Domingo, he said:

"This country would certainly decline to go to war to prevent a foreign government from collecting" on defaulted debts; and since a temporary occupation by a European Power might turn into a permanent occupation, "the only escape from these alternatives may at some time be that we must ourselves undertake to bring about some arrangement by which so much as possible of a just obligation shall be paid."

In the meantime the Panama Canal route had been decided upon, and the treaty signed with the Republic of Panama, and in his message of 1904 President Roosevelt stated his corollary to the Monroe Doctrine:

"Chronic wrongdoing, or an impotence which results in a general loosening of the ties of civilized society, may in America as elsewhere ultimately require intervention by some civilized power, and in the Western Hemisphere the adherence of the United States to the Monroe Doctrine may force the United States, however reluctantly, in flagrant cases of such wrongdoing or impotence, to the exercise of an international police power."

Whatever may have been the actual circumstances and the contributing motives, it was under this Roosevelt corollary of the international police power that there took place the intervention of 1905 in Santo Domingo, and the interventions by Secretary Knox in Nicaragua and Haiti which culminated in the treaties of 1911.

This assumption of the right to police the Caribbean grew out of the vital national interest created in that region by the construction of the Panama Canal. The American system of defense was based on the Canal, and it followed from this new fact that the United States could no longer tolerate European naval activity in that strategic area. There followed from this same fact the establishment of a series of naval bases at Key West, Guantanamo, Samana Bay, Mole St. Nicholas, in Porto Rico, in the Virgin Islands, in the Corn Islands of Nicaragua, and in Fonseca Bay on the Pacific side. With this development the United States could no longer tolerate political disorder in the countries involved in its naval defense. It could not tolerate the threat of

European intervention in case of disorder, and it could not tolerate disorder which threatened the security of its own strategic system. From this point it was but a short step to the theory that the United States must insure itself in the Caribbean region against supposedly unfriendly governments. It was this point which was reached apparently in the present affair in Nicaragua.

Thus in a hundred years the Monroe Doctrine evolved from the simple prohibition of further colonization through the assumption of an international police power in the Caribbean to an insistence that governments in that region shall be, not only orderly, but friendly to the interests of the United States. This growth of American policy is however an evolution out of the principle of national security, and each new phase of it is consistent with that principle. That other motives played their part, that private interests may at times have created the situation, or made themselves the instruments and the beneficiaries, need not be denied. I shall not discuss here this aspect of what is popularly known as "Dollar Diplomacy," because when in these disputed cases the United States Government acted, it appealed always, and I believe sincerely, to the principle of national security.

It is important to bear this in mind because in the present dispute with Mexico the government is appealing to a new and radically different principle. What that principle is, what its acceptance

may imply, is a matter of real concern to the United
States and to the rest of the world.

III

After the fall of Porfirio Diaz there was a revolution in Mexico which was essentially different from
the ordinary Latin-American civil commotion. It
was not a mere brawl between the Ins and the Outs,
but a national upheaval against the landed gentry,
against clericalism, and against the foreign conces-
sionaire who was rapidly acquiring the richest natural resources of the country. An *ancien régime*
was violently overturned amidst considerable disorder, much irregularity, plenty of selfishness
and dishonesty and inefficiency and floods of revolutionary rhetoric. This revolution, which is loosely
called bolshevik and is often ascribed by careless
writers to the Russian Communists, was fought out
and consummated while the Tsar was still on the
throne of Russia. The new Mexican Constitution
which embodies the results of the revolution went
into effect on May 1, 1917, over six months before
Lenin seized the government in Russia.

Whatever name is to be given to it, the fact is
indisputable that the Mexican revolution arose out
of Mexican conditions in an effort to correct Mexican evils, and that it takes its place historically with
that series of nationalist uprisings which from China
to India, from Egypt to Morocco, offer so profound

a challenge to the supremacy of the Western Empires, and so deep a riddle to their statesmanship. One persistent motive in these uprisings is the desire to assert the national independence and the dignity of an inferior race. The whole spirit of extraterritorial privileges in all its forms is therefore under attack—the whole system of special courts, codes, concessions which give the foreigner a status in these countries superior to that of the native.

This nationalism inevitably comes into conflict with the vested rights of foreigners. These rights have a varied history. Most of them were probably acquired legitimately, or at least in good faith under the old régime; some of them, enough of them perhaps to stand out as horrible examples, may not have been so legitimately acquired even under the old system. Yet no matter how they were acquired they represent after the lapse of years a large investment of honest capital, much hard work, and in the case of rare and essential natural resources, a considerable national interest to the people at home. There is then a real conflict between the nationalism of the country and the acquired rights of the foreigner.

It is this conflict which the United States Government has been trying to deal with ever since the Mexican Constitution was established in 1917, and even earlier. There is a long record of diplomatic notes on the subject extending back to the time when the Convention of Queretaro was still drafting the

Constitution. The fundamental point of protest is Article XXVII, which declared the subsoil of Mexico the property of the nation. This famous article embodies the purposes and the slogans of the revolution; in the eyes of Mexicans it represents a recovery by the nation of property that belonged to it, except for a brief period under President Diaz and then only in respect to some minerals, ever since the title passed from the King of Spain to the States of the independent Republic of Mexico.

The Mexican revolutionists, however, have had the prudence to recognize that the acquired rights of foreigners could not be wiped out. Their courts have declared that Article XXVII is not retroactive, and in their legislation which enacts Article XXVII they have made provision for the continued use of such property in the subsoil as was legitimately acquired before 1917. Whether this provision is substantially just or not, and whether the Mexican courts fairly interpret former Mexican law, is fiercely disputed by most of the American oil companies, and their claim is supported by the State Department. Into the merits of that dispute I shall not attempt to enter here. My concern is with the doctrine upon which the American contention is based. That is much more important in the long run than the immediate dispute about the oil properties, for the doctrine we now announce, and may in the end establish, will govern our future relations not only with Mexico but with any country in which acquired rights are affected by a radical change of social policy.

Mr. Hughes, when he was Secretary of State, laid down the following rule in relation to Latin-America:

"Each state may have its code of laws in accordance with its conception of domestic policy, but rights acquired under its laws by citizens of another state it is under an international obligation *appropriately* to recognize."

Under Secretary Kellogg this doctrine seems to have lost whatever qualification there may have been in Mr. Hughes's mind when he used the word "appropriately."   Mr. Kellogg's doctrine as laid down in the series of notes between July and November, 1926, was that Mexico did not have the power to diminish in any way a legal title acquired before 1917 whether or not the change of title inflicted a substantial loss upon the owner.   Mr. Kellogg, if I understand him correctly, contends that a title to property once acquired must be left intact in letter, in spirit, and in substance for all time to come. And President Coolidge, if I understand the Official Spokesman correctly, has added that the rights of a vested interest to an unchangeable title against acts of the sovereign are so clear under international law that it is not even an arbitrable question.   This is a radical and unqualified position, allowing no room for compromise, as does Mr. Hughes's principle qualified by the word "appropriately." The Kellogg doctrine does not, in principle at least, allow Mexico to confirm the oil companies in the use of their lands while maintaining the theory or the fiction that the title vests in the nation.

Whether or not Secretary Kellogg would adhere to so strict a dogma if Mexico offered a better bargain to the oil companies, I do not know. But it is certain that the rigorous form in which the American claim has been formulated has produced a head-on collision between two irreconcilable principles. They are the principle of national sovereignty and the principle of acquired rights. The doctrine for which Secretary Kellogg is now contending is in effect that a right to property is an inalienable right which no government can ever impair, that it is superior under international law to the right of sovereignty, and that when the acts of the sovereign conflict with the vested rights of foreign property holders these acts of the sovereign are null and void under international law. Mr. Kellogg has argued that the wrong done by the legislation which carries the Mexican Constitution into effect is such that it cannot be righted by reparation for the material damage suffered by American property holders in specific cases. He has rejected the Mexican offer to make reparation if damages could be proved. He has argued that the wrong is too deep to be remedied by the payment of damages, even assuming that Mexico would or could pay the damages which might be assessed against her. For an act of the sovereign which diminishes a title to property inflicts an injury for which no compensation after the fact can be sufficient. The act itself is confiscatory and strikes at the root of international law as Mr. Kellogg understands the law of nations.

Just where or when it became the law of nations that the sovereign has not the power to affect the established title to property has never been explained by the State Department. For if this were the law of nations then legislation anywhere in the world, including the United States, is subject to review not only by the highest domestic courts, but by the Foreign Offices of aliens whose rights are affected. The United States Supreme Court has for generations been deciding cases in which the question was whether an act of Congress or of one of the state legislatures was "confiscatory." In a long series of decisions it has sanctioned legislation which drastically diminished the free use of legitimately acquired property. Under these decisions the railroads and other public utilities have been regulated, the use of real estate has been hedged with restrictions like the rent laws and the zoning laws, employers have been subjected to all kinds of "welfare" legislation. Americans have differed greatly among themselves as to whether these laws were wise, and immense lawsuits have been carried through the courts to determine whether they were confiscatory. But I doubt whether any American ever dreamed that after the Supreme Court had rendered its decision, a British subject who owned railway securities or New York City real estate could carry the case to the British Foreign Office for an ultimate review and decision.

If this were the law of nations it would mean that each nation possessed a veto on the legislature and courts of every other nation in so far as its nationals had rights that were affected. This theory that the vested rights of aliens are immutable, and superior to the acts of the sovereign, would mean, if it were accepted, that in proportion to the size of alien holdings, a nation's social developments would be frozen in *statu quo*. If this were the law of nations then no people which cherished its independence could ever again permit foreigners to acquire property. For such property, once acquired, would be forever removed from national control. The foreigner with his property would be above the law of the country, and his rights would be determined not by the sovereign power but by an alien Foreign Office.

IV

It is altogether unlikely that Secretary Kellogg would wish to commit this country to the full implication of his doctrine. It would lead us into great difficulties. Against a strong power the doctrine would be unenforceable except by resort to war. If, for example, in the course of the next few years the

British Government decides to nationalize the coal industry, it will not ask the consent of our State Department. American owners of coal properties in England will have to accept the same terms which are offered to English owners, and the terms will not be, I venture to suggest, a matter even for diplomatic discussion. The terms offered to landlords in Ireland were not reviewed by alien Foreign Offices, nor would the terms laid down by Congress be subject to review in case some day it decided to reorganize our chaotic coal industry. Any strong nation would take the position that where there was no discrimination against the foreigner or between foreigners, where there was no taking of property from aliens and giving it to its own nationals, where the action arose from a considered policy in the national interest, where in fact there was no intention to expropriate without some practicable substitute, where its own courts (or even an international tribunal) were open to hear proof of damages, there could be no ground for diplomatic interference. Mr. Kellogg has taken the contrary position in relation to Mexico. The seriousness of his position is not merely that it constitutes a threat to good relations with Mexico, but that it portends the possibility that on this continent at least the United States may set itself up as the opponent of national aspiration and social development.

No one can quarrel with the State Department for giving the oil companies every assistance in making a good bargain with the Mexican Government, nor in seeing to it that they are dealt with reasonably and without prejudice. But there is a very real danger in setting up as an unqualified dogma the theory that American investments in Latin-America are in fact extra-territorial, and that the State Department may on its own authority exercise the powers of the Supreme Court under the Fourteenth Amendment over all the governments of this hemisphere. The responsibilities we should incur under such a doctrine would be infinite. For as our investments grew the State Department would find itself acting both as attorney for interests affected by legislation in Latin-America, and as final court of review as well.

With this doctrine established in our foreign policy we could hardly expect to win the good will of the awakening nationalists of the Latin countries. They would find us confronting them whenever they contemplated a change in their social policy. And unless the State Department chose to play favorites, giving to the oil companies in Mexico a kind of support which it was not willing to give other American interests elsewhere, it would have to entangle itself in every political conflict which had economic consequences, anywhere south of the Rio Grande.

Rightly or wrongly the Latin peoples would regard this intimate interference as a threat to their independence, and we might expect anti-Americanism to become part of the creed of all Latin patriots, professional and otherwise. Nor would European traders in South America be above the temptation to point out the implications of this Kellogg Doctrine, assuming that the Latin peoples, already sufficiently suspicious, should somehow miss the implications. Nor is it unlikely, were we to deal with Latin-America in too heavy-handed a way, that the larger nations there would feel impelled to turn once more toward Europe, seeking a support there which would eventually restore some kind of balance of power in this hemisphere. . . .

V

To these more remote and imponderable considerations men will give weight in accordance with their temperaments and their wisdom. The immediate question before the American people is whether they wish to erect the doctrine of immutability of vested rights into a cardinal principle of their foreign policy. This is the great question which overshadows the Mexican dispute. It arises, as has been pointed out, from the conflict between the growth of capital investment in backward countries and the awakening of a national spirit in these countries. The Kellogg Doctrine, taken as it has been stated in the correspondence with Mexico, holds that vested rights are unchangeable in the face of a nation's development. Such a doctrine, applied so absolutely, means an irreconcilable collision between the power of this country and the will of its neighbors.

The task of statesmanship is to avert irreconcilable collisions and to find ways of adjusting conflicting interests. That ought not to be beyond the bounds of possibility. It ought not to be impossible to protect the substantial interests of American capital abroad without challenging the right of other nations to adopt such social regulation as seems good to them. Business is a much more flexible thing than the conservative theorist is ready to believe. It cannot be irreparably injured without injury to the nation which attacks it. If Mexico really tried to injure the oil business, the worst damage would recoil upon Mexico herself. There are considerations to which the statesman can afford to pay attention, and they suggest that the solution of the problem, which is as real as it is delicate, will probably be found best by seeking a *modus vivendi,* respecting the national pride of sensitive peoples, and refraining, so far as it is humanly possible to avoid so great a temptation, from enunciating great general principles.

In the last analysis the security of American investments abroad must rest, as Mr. Dwight Morrow has pointed out, on the faith of the borrowing nations. They must believe that American capital profits them, and is consistent with their own national interest. If they do not believe this, pressure which forces them to act contrary to their convictions can give only temporary advantages to American business men. The victory on one point can be won only at the cost of arousing a general ill will against American capital and the American Government. Such a general ill will is more threatening to the security not only of capital but of the nation than any one Latin policy however inconvenient, however ill-considered. And nothing would be so certain to arouse still further this ill will as the realization in Latin-America that the United States had adopted a policy, conceived in the spirit of Metternich, which would attempt to guarantee vested rights against social progress as the Latin peoples conceive it.

April, 1927.

EMPIRE: THE DAYS OF OUR NONAGE
ARE OVER

ALL the world thinks of the United States to-day as an empire, except the people of the United States. We shrink from the word "empire," and insist that it should not be used to describe the dominion we exercise from Alaska to the Philippines, from Cuba to Panama, and beyond. We feel that there ought to be some other name for the civilizing work which we do so reluctantly in these backward countries. I think the reluctance is genuine. I feel morally certain that an overwhelming majority of our citizens do not wish to rule other peoples, and that there is no hypocrisy in the pained protest which rises whenever a Latin-American or a European speaks of us as imperialistic. We do not feel ourselves to be imperialists as we understand that word. We are not conscious of any such desire for expansion as the Fascists, for example, proclaim every day. We have learned to think of empires as troublesome and as immoral, and to admit that we have an empire still seems to most Americans like admitting that they have gone out into a wicked world and there lost their political chastity.

Our sensitiveness on this point can be seen by an incident which happened recently in connection with that venerable book of reference, the "Almanach de Gotha." Here, in this social register of the royal and princely families of Europe, there appears, as of 1924, a list of American "protectorates." They are Cuba, Dominican Republic, Haiti, Liberia, and Panama. Now there can be no doubt that Washington exercises as much real authority in these countries, with the possible exception of Liberia, as London does in many parts of the dependent empire. Yet the "Almanach de Gotha's" innocent use of the word "protectorates" was immediately protested by Mr. James Brown Scott, Director of the Division of International Law of the Carnegie Endowment for International Peace. Mr. Scott pointed out, quite accurately, that the United States had never officially admitted the existence of any protectorates, and that Secretaries of State had again and again announced, as Mr. Hughes did in 1923, that "we recognize the equality of the American Republics, their equal rights under the law of nations."

I do not know what the "Almanach de Gotha" is going to do about this, but it is certain that the rest of the world will continue to think of us as an empire. Foreigners pay little attention to what we say. They observe what we do. We on the other hand think of what we feel. And the result is that we go on creating what mankind calls an empire while we continue to believe quite sincerely that it is not an empire because it does not feel to us the way we imagine an empire ought to feel.

What the rest of the world sees is that after we had, in the years from 1803 to 1853, rounded out the territory of continental United States by purchase and by conquest, there was a pause in our expansion; that this was followed by the purchase of Alaska in 1867, the annexation of Hawaii in 1898, the obtaining possession of the Philippines and Porto Rico, and, in a different form, of Cuba as a result of the Spanish War. From that time on the expansion of American influence in the Caribbean and the West Indies has widened until there is hardly a country in that whole region which has not seen an American intervention. In an article which was printed in *The*

New Republic Professor Shephard of Columbia University has counted the following separate military interventions in the Caribbean between 1898 and 1927. In Cuba, four; in Panama, five; in the Dominican Republic, five; in Nicaragua, six (the last still in progress); Haiti, one, still in progress; Mexico, two; Honduras, six; Costa Rica, one; Colombia, one. Scattered all over the Caribbean are American High Commissioners and other officials, working under treaties, loan agreements and the like.

For all practical purposes, we control the foreign relations of all the Caribbean countries; not one of them could enter into serious relations abroad without our consent. We control their relations with each other, as was shown recently when the State Department thought it an outrage because Mexico recognized one President of Nicaragua when we had recognized another. We exercise the power of life and death over their governments in that no government can survive if we refuse it recognition. We help in many of these countries to decide what they call their elections, and we do not hesitate, as we have done recently in Mexico, to tell them what kind of constitution we think they ought to have.

Whatever we may choose to call it, this is what the world at large calls an empire, or at least an empire in the making. Admitting that the word has an unpleasant connotation, nevertheless it does seem as if the time had come for us to look the whole thing squarely in the face and to stop trying to deceive ourselves. We shall persuade nobody abroad by our words. We shall merely acquire a reputation for hypocrisy while we stumble unconsciously into the cares and the perils of empire. Now an unconscious empire has dangers that may be even greater than a conscious one. There is nothing to be gained by talking about one thing and doing another.

The only effect of this refusal to admit that we are assuming imperial responsibilities is to turn over the management of our empire to business men with a personal share in it, and to our second-rate and least experienced diplomats. We have men in the diplomatic service who have had some experience in Latin-America, but as soon as they have learned enough to be any good they manage to have themselves promoted to a European capital where the plumbing is better. Look at the result. There is no more important post in the State Department to-day than that of the Chief of the Division of Mexican Affairs. It is filled by a gentleman whose name I shall suppress because there is no need to use it. Now note the diplomatic career of this official (as given by *Who's Who*) and see how carefully he has been trained for his responsibilities in regard to Mexico:

Private secretary, American Ambassador to Japan, 1908-1909;
Third secretary, American Embassy at Paris, 1909-1910;

With the Division of Latin-American Affairs, Washington, 1910-1911;

Secretary of the American Legation, Managua, Chargé d' Affaires, 1911-1912;

Lisbon, secretary of Legation and Chargé d' Affaires, 1912;

Second secretary of the Embassy, Rio de Janeiro, 1912-1914;

Secretary of the Legation, Christiania, February, 1914 (Chargé d' Affaires);

Secretary to the American delegation to the International Conference, Spitzbergen, June, 1914;

Second secretary of the Embassy, London, 1914-1917, first secretary, 1917-1919;

First secretary of the Legation, The Hague and Chargé d' Affaires, 1919-1920;

Counsellor of the American Embassy at Rome, 1920-1924;

And Chief of the Mexican Affairs since 1924.

Here is a trained diplomat as we understand the term, but for what has he been trained? The nearest he ever got to a post in Mexico was to be in Nicaragua in 1911-1912, and on the basis of this intensive and intimate knowledge of Mexico, her people and her problems, he acts as adviser on, and interpreter of, dispatches from Mexico for the enlightenment of Secretary Kellogg, who has never had a post in Mexico, and to President Coolidge, who has certainly never had one either. There may be some one in the State Department who knows Mexico intimately and at firsthand, but if there is such a person he is not Chief of the Mexican Division.

I have not described this situation in order to cast

aspersions upon this official who may be a useful member of the service. But the situation in which he finds himself is preposterous. It is preposterous that at a critical time the Chief of the Mexican Division should be a man who never had a post in Mexico, and has apparently spent only two years of a busy life, and then fifteen years ago, in any Caribbean country. It is not his fault. It is the fault of a system under which the Caribbean countries, the theater of our empire, are dealt with absent-mindedly, in a left-handed way, without realization of the responsibilities involved.

The refusal to recognize what we are doing in the Caribbean, the persistent use of meaningless, high-sounding generalities about "equality" in lieu of direct discussion of our increasing penetration and control, has prevented the formation of a body of intelligent and disinterested opinion. When something happens in the Caribbean, the only voices heard are those of the oil men, the fruit men, mining men, bankers on one side, and the outraged voices of the Gladstone liberals on the other. The debate is conducted by the hard-boiled and soft-hearted. There is no opinion which is both hard-headed and far-seeing. The effect on policy is bad: the hard-boiled interest works continuously, and the rather amateurish officials in the State Department who are assigned to these duties are unable to cope with it. They do not know enough. They are not strong enough. They have no sufficient incentive to set themselves up against the powerful interests which are telling them what they ought to do. So usually the situation is developed without the check of public criticism until it reaches a climax where marines have to be used. Then the soft-hearted people roll over in bed and wake up. There is a great outcry about imperialism, and the policy of the government becomes confused and vacillating. After a while the soft-hearted clamor subsides, the normal relations are resumed between the hard-boiled interests and the ambitious young diplomats with a career to be made.

There can be no remedy for this until Americans make up their minds to recognize the fact that they are no longer a virginal republic in a wicked world, but they are themselves a world power, and one of the most portentous which has appeared in the history of mankind. When they have let that truth sink in, have digested it, and appraised it, they will cast aside the old phrases which conceal the reality, and as a fully adult nation, they will begin to prepare themselves for the part that their power and their position compel them to play.

April, 1927.

SECOND BEST STATESMEN

I

Mr. Bernard Shaw has convinced himself that the art of civilization is too long for short-lived men. What can be expected, he asks, from a breed of novices and flappers who die off when they are still politically adolescent, and temporize with every great issue because they will not live long enough to care whether is is settled or not? Is it true, as Mr. Shaw says, that we are ruled by freshmen who will never mature?

My own opinion is that we do not know whether it is true or not. We have not any conception, I believe, of the present powers of man, short-lived as he is. We have a hint of his enormous mechanical ingenuity, of his astounding physical courage, of his unbelievable patience. But of his latent capacity for bringing order out of the tohubohu of human relations we know very little because he is not seriously trying. We have learned almost to think that satisfaction with the second best is a mark of good humor and wisdom, that it is gauche not to discount the pretensions of all public characters, not to conclude almost any discussion of public affairs with an "Ah, well! they're pretty good fellows, I suppose, and doing the best they know."

Now, we may all be pretty good fellows, but in the art of civilization we are emphatically not doing the best we know how. Our public men are in fact quite dismayed, when they have the leisure and candor to stop and think. Again and again, in critical matters, they find themselves doing what they know to be foolish. As they reflect they are amazed when they watch themselves upholding policies they know will not work, making promises they know they cannot keep, purveying cheap and second-rate goods which privately they despise, and evading to-day or postponing for posterity what should be dealt with at once. For real criticism of the statesman you do not need to go to Mr. Shaw's Burge and Lubin; you have only to go to the statesmen themselves, when they are off duty and are not talking for publication.

You may come away from such a talk still convinced that man is congenitally incapable of civilization. But you are just as likely to come away feeling elated at the candor of which men are capable in private, and depressed by their apparent inability to let their best insight govern their public life. That, at least, is the feeling I have brought away with me from many journalistic interviews. And only, I think, by recalling that public men lead this double life, can you account for some of the inexplicable devotion they so often arouse. The thick-and-thin followers see the private character rather than the public personage. Did they see only the carefully constructed façades they, too, would be discouraged. For public men, in spite of their press agents, usually put their worst foot forward in public life. But those who are behind the façade can like the man for the possibilities he really possesses. Those out front have to judge by his display. After a while, perhaps after prolonged contemplation of a performance like that of Congress with the bonus, they are bound to think with Mr. Shaw that all public characters are a total loss and no insurance.

And yet, what if it were possible, taking men as they are, to liberate the possibilities that in moments of candor are revealed to the devoted? We do not know what would happen. We know a little of what has happened in the conquest of nature when this liberation took place—when men shook themselves free of their own tabus. In the physical sciences little remains of the disproportion between what a discoverer really thinks and what in the interests of his reputation he sees fit to tell the world. There it is not considered wiser and better form and more mellow to be rather inaccurate and decently secretive. Why, then, should there be a cult of the second-rate in our public relations?

II

Mr. Shaw thinks that man practices this cult because he has not a sufficient stake in the world. According to what he calls, in "Back to Methuselah," the Gospel of the Brothers Barnabas, man's attitude toward civilization is that of a transient and untidy tenant without interest in the upkeep or improvement of the property. Others think that the root of the trouble lies in "capitalism"; some think it lies in commercialism; some in Puritanism; some in the great tide of immigration; some in the primitive state of our knowledge; some in the inherent difficulty of the subject matter of the social sciences.

I think the argument can be pursued for a while on different lines. For grant that it is desirable to breed and educate and select better men, grant everything the eugenicist and educator and creative evolu-

tionist demand; still it is possible to argue from the
fact that there is such a gap between public and
private character, that this world would soon be a
better place to live in if every one who exercises
authority or helps to shape public opinion acted
according to such lights as he now has. It is possible to argue that the improvement following the
closing of the gap would be cumulative.

Very easily one can talk nonsense in these matters,
but personally I am convinced that almost no one to-
day who deals with large electorates, with great cir-
culations, with anonymous publics, is wholly without a kind of inner stultification.   Something it
seems has obtruded between the individual and the
public which acts as a depressant and self-censor
upon a candid first-rate relationship. In their public dealings, most men are much less than themselves. They assume that a certain insincerity is
necessary to success, that a little less than common
sense is appropriate, that the best is the enemy of
the better. They have the attitude of a nurse to
a patient. They involve themselves deeply in considerations of manner and tact. They become so
preoccupied with the eternal question of how to
"put something across," and how much to ladle out
at one dose, and how good is the digestion of the
public, that their own interest in the subject matter
is diverted and distracted. In their anxiety about
the sugar-coating, they forget the pill. Their own
powers of invention and judgment are starved

through disuse, while their powers of promotion and salesmanship grow constantly more elaborate.

The fashionable thing to do in this connection is to pronounce the phrase "herd instinct" with a sense of finality. At the moment, these are magic words yielding glamour and ironical relief. The leaders huddle with the herd. They are afraid to be alone as the crowd is afraid of people who are different. There is nothing to do about it but repeat "herd instinct" whenever your feelings need expression.

Or if you do not share this biological fatalism, you can insist with good three-dimensional invective that man is naturally timid and lazy, and that he will always take the easiest way. If the quickest way to fame and fortune is to catch votes, collect audiences, and increase the circulation by saying faintly insincere and second-rate things, Adam will indulge. Man will take that way. You can preach against it. You can exhort him to "the search and expectation of greatest and exactest things," but your success will in the main be negative. You may put a brake on the deterioration of standards. You may stir up that conscience in the community which does somehow manage to set a lowest limit for the panderer. You can do little more because the conscience of the community deals with the minimum. When it comes to setting standards of excellence, preaching is likely to be feeble, rhetorical, and ineffective.

For there is something that conflicts with an

unexamined premise of our culture in a sermon aimed to incite men to pursue their highest good. We ought to look for that premise. I believe that the trouble can be located: that what some call the herd instinct, and others natural laziness and timidity, has surreptitiously acquired the sanction of conscience in democracy; and that the older conceptions of duty, honor, and excellence are undercut by a myth that passes for the latest science and the most modern conception of democracy. I believe this myth is partly a survival from the days when democracy was fighting for existence and improvising a creed, and partly confusion due to the absence of a really friendly and drastic criticism of democratic ideas; that it has no more to do with the intrinsic virtues of democracy than Alexandrine speculation had to do with the teachings of Jesus; and that it has no more to do with the substance of popular government than the medieval picture of the heavens had with the Gospels.

A distracting error has worked itself into the democratic tradition which is corrupting to the will because it sanctifies the cult of the second best.

III

The man who in a roomful of up-to-the-minute people ventured to use the word "reason" in connection with public affairs would soon discover that he was naïvely endangering his reputation. There would be an embarrassed silence, almost as awkward as if he had smuggled himself into a congress of scientists and was asserting that the earth is flat. Savvy Barnabas, who is Mr. Shaw's incarnation of an advanced intellect, would probably bounce out of the room choking with laughter. Or if she stayed long enough to argue, she would tell the apostle of reason that apparently his brain is upholstered with red plush, and, therefore, he does not know that the function of reason in politics is to find pretexts for realizing the wishes of men. She would insist that a wish clothed in a reason constitutes an interest, and that interests are the only guide in public affairs.

Savvy is proud of this discovery. She regards it as a touchstone for telling fossils from freemen. It seems to work well. She can employ it with devastating effect upon academicians whose habits of thought hardened before the discovery was generally known. And since there are still many of these academicians left, and since there is even a renewal of the supply from certain centers of learning, and since these unemancipated people write a greater percentage of the books and make a greater percentage of the speeches than they are entitled to make according to the population statistics, Savvy is under the impression that they speak the accepted doctrine of the great mass of the people. Because her battleground is among the books and the reviews, she does not know that the real intellectual battleground has shifted, that fact has run far ahead of theory, and that she is a good half turn behind in the cycle of thought. Observing that the conservative academicians arrive at much the same conclusions about the Republican Party as her uncles, Savvy thinks these academicians do the thinking for the community, and goes for them head on.

But Savvy is mistaken. Her own doctrine is far more popular as a working philosophy than that of this older generation. She is, without knowing it, rushing eagerly to the support of the victors. For, except among a few authors and professors, the doctrine of interests is triumphant in everyday life.

Modern teaching about the rôle of the interests has been transfigured much as was the theory of evolution two generations ago. What was intended as a mere statement of probable fact has been twisted into an absolute moral precept. In the case of evolution, the idea that change is unending was hastily moralized into the belief that change for the better was inevitable. Then it followed that to-morrow was inevitably better than yesterday. And merely to come after was an improvement on what had gone before. All the generations since Aristotle stood on each others' shoulders, and he who would stand on ours could almost touch the sky.

The theory of interests was at first as neutral, as much beyond good and evil, as evolution. The discoverers claimed nothing for it but that they had

observed in somewhat greater detail than people
had ever observed it before that a wish was father to
most thoughts. They taught that most of the time
when men imagined they were acting on reason they
were in truth finding reasons for acting as they
desired. Few of them claimed that men could never
act on reason, for such an admission would have
tainted their own inquiries. Certainly they did not
say that men could not, or ought not to try to follow
reason, but only that, more often than was currently
believed, reason was an apologist and an advocate
rather than a counsellor and a judge.

The new technique for going under the other
fellow's skin, and exposing him in the act of ration-
alizing his impulses, satisfied Savvy's lust of battle.
The technique came to her at first or second hand
from the writings of James, Bergson, and Freud;
and their heresy became her orthodoxy. Because
the anti-intellectualists had been fighting men, as well
as scientists, all of them wrote with an eye on their
academic colleagues, and they stated their position
in a series of polemics against opponents who were
dogmatic rationalists. Savvy has inherited the
polemics along with the doctrine. And, if the truth
be told, it is the polemics that she likes best. She
imagines, anyhow, that she is championing the
newest truth by brandishing the sticks which men
old enough to be her grandfather used in order to
beat their grandfathers. She has not realized that
she is thrashing a straw man. She has not waked

up to the fact that, however hard-shelled the opposition of scholars may have been, the new knowledge spread like a prairie fire. Often it assumed strange shapes that would have horrified the pioneers; but it passed quickly into usage, and was acclaimed with shouts of joy by every one who was glad he could now believe that to be timid and timeserving was to be at once ultra-modern and scientific and an advanced democrat.

IV

For by a twist in the association of ideas, the theory of interests coalesced with that of government by consent of the governed. The statement in scientific jargon that the wish is father to the thought amalgamated with the faith that the will of the people should be supreme. Out of this confusion emerged the conviction that the wish which is father to the thought should be supreme in politics, the newspapers, the movies, and the theater. In consequence, the people who take the doctrine very literally go about by day, and make sure they have pencil and pad within reach when they are in bed at night, so that they may listen in for their impulses, and obey them. They move on tiptoe so that they may overhear the voice of the unconscious. Politicians speak their real thoughts in whispers for fear of creating commotion in the ether that might interfere with their deciphering the wishes of the public. The final answer to any proposal is that the people do not want it; the final excuse for anything is that the people want what they want when they want it.

In our world this has become the chief substitute for the old architecture of heaven and hell, the ancient springs of revelation, the oracles and the sacred books, and the authoritative code of morals which they sanctioned. To a limited extent the older views survive, but they seem clearly archaic and are threatened with extinction. For behind this new attitude there is a great pride, a great sense of emancipation from ancient error. So great a pride is it, so great a sense of freedom, that the faults of the old are sufficient to float the new. The doctrine of watchful waiting, of mysterious popular guidance, of purely receptive and purely passive leadership, has an air about it of democratic humility, of unpretentiousness, of nobly serving great things. What is man on the scale of time? A mere spokesman, a transmitter, a dictograph.

It is quite easy to become mystical on the subject. You can say that out of the vasty deeps of our modern minds, out of the eternal caverns of the unconscious, out of the collective super-soul and over-soul, profounder than reason, impregnated with the everlasting memories of the race, instinctive with primal knowledge and heavy laden with immemorial wisdom, comes the will of the people. Not your half-hearted views and mine, not our compound of prejudices and headlines and inattention, but something other and utter. And all the politician or

the editor has to do is to wait and listen and strain
his ear, and he will know just what to do about the
sales tax and the bonus, ship subsidies and the tariff,
reparations and the integrity of China.

Thus, by sleight-of-hand, popular government
embraced a mythology. Beginning with a theory
based on the vision of a very simple village community where every one knew everybody else's character and affairs, and inspired by a high sense of
human equality, the democrat found himself in an
unmanageable civilization. No man's wisdom
seemed to be great enough for the task. A somewhat more mystical wisdom was necessary. But
about the steadiness of the supply of that wisdom
he still had inner doubt. Then came the doctrine
of interests to relieve the tension. It was said,
apparently on the highest scientific authority, that
all men instinctively pursued their interests; that
their reason need not be dealt with because it was a
mere pretext for their wishes; and that all you had
to do was to probe for the interests of the people,
and you were in touch with reality.

But as a practical matter, it was not at all easy
to tell offhand what were the interests which the will
of the people expressed. The popular will had a
way of formulating itself in abstract nouns like
Justice, Right, Honor, Americanism. It proved to
be rather a 'puzzle, therefore, just how the leaders
were to detect the interests which the unconscious
collective soul was uttering. At that critical moment

the sophists stepped in, and by manipulating the double meaning of "interest" they laid to rest the scruples of conscience.

It happens that "interest" may mean either the feeling of concern or the fact of being concerned. The difference is often very great. A child has, for example, a very great interest in his father's business affairs. They will determine many of his opportunities in life. But the child is not in the least interested in any discussion of his father's business. Similarly, the people of the United States have an enormous interest in the settlement of German reparations, but they were far more interested in reading about the wedding gown of the Princess Mary. When the Reparations Commission makes a decision, no courier takes an airplane for the nearest ocean greyhound, carrying the full text in a water-tight packet specially designed to float, and casts it overboard where a fast destroyer can pick it up, and rush it to Boston Harbor twenty-four hours and eighteen minutes before the ocean greyhound docks in New York. We are not sufficiently interested in some of our biggest interests to take that much trouble.

But by confusing the two meanings of the word "interest," the sophists could satisfy themselves that the degree of interest felt was a true index in a democracy of the amount of interest at stake. They could pose as servants of the public by identifying interest subjectively felt with interest as an objective

reality.   They could confuse what the public seems
to demand now with what the public in the long
run needs.   It is a deep and corrupting ambiguity.
It is to say that a taste for marshmallows is the
clue to a diet.

V

No such grossly obvious play upon words would,
of course, have found wide acceptance, were there
not in the background a powerful will to believe.
The desire to think that our wishes are instinctively
directed to the satisfaction of our own best interests,
and of society's, has grown as the older systems of
authority in government, religion, and morals have
disintegrated.   In a world complicated beyond their
powers, men who were deprived of external guidance
have had to fall back upon themselves.   But on what
selves were they to fall back? The traditional Higher
Self, consisting of a code of Duty and Rights and
Purposes, had disintegrated with the institutions of
which it was a part.

For a brief time, the individual reason acting
deductively on its own premises was elected to carry
the burden.   But it did not take long to discover
that individual reason working on accidental
premises in people's minds was more often than not
a mere intellectualization of their hopes and fears.
Its authority collapsed at the approach of the
analytical psychologists.   But there remained the
sheer human necessity of believing in something that

could be trusted as a guide to conduct. What was that something to be? It could not be a revealed religion nor a revealed political system; it could not be the individual reason acting alone, for that was now understood to take its direction not from the facts of the environment but from the stresses and urgencies of each person. Apparently, the instinctive needs and appetites were the governing forces of human life.

And then, because we all have a tendency to worship whatever is powerful and certain, the cult of instinct was taken up by nineteenth-century liberalism. Since it had been demonstrated more or less convincingly that most of our reasoning and most of our beliefs were dominated by desire, men proclaimed that desire was the utimate reality. Being ultimate, it must be ultimately right. Being ultimately right, it must be intelligent. Being intelligent, it must be capable of expressing itself. And therefore in reverse order, the intensity and quantity of whatever was expressed was the sign of an intelligent pursuit of what was ultimately right.

This is, I think, a true statement of the prevailing belief about human nature. Few hold it in a pure form or act upon it all the time. The older ideas survive to modify it somewhat in practice, and there is also a check upon it in certain of the newer schools of thought. But the realm over which the doctrine presides is, nevertheless, immense. It determines the characteristically "modern" attitude in innumerable fields of activity.

The popular modern theory of the instincts is a vestibule to several different conflicting schools of thought. It leads, for example, to many naïve theories about the economic interpretation of politics. Usually, these theories assume that men group themselves more or less infallibly by economic classes, and that the programs they adopt express their economic interests. But is there any evidence for thinking that this rule holds? Do people never vote foolishly, do they never vote for laws that injure them? Is the fact that a group asks for a measure any evidence that a measure is really to its advantage? It seems to me clear that it is no evidence at all. And if it is no evidence, it follows that the word "self-interest," which has such an air of reality about it, has no reality. It is used with assurance only by people who are confused by the two meanings of the word "interest," and who imagine that the measures in which a group of workingmen, or a farmers' bloc, or a manufacturers' association happen to be interested, are equivalent to a policy which will in fact further their economic interests.

VI

The cult of instinct has turned out to be an illusion. And if we read more carefully what modern psychology actually teaches, we can see readily enough why it is an illusion. The instincts are not stimulated to activity, as perhaps they were in primitive ages, by a true picture of the relevant environment in which they must find their satisfaction, but oftener than not in our civilization by quite false fictions, accidentally encountered or deliberately devised. They are not set in motion by obvious truth, and the action to which they are habituated has no necessary connection with the end desired. For this reason it is impossible in the modern world to trust instinct alone, once it is seen that our instincts are not in gear with the facts, and that they are not equipped by habit with a knowledge of ways and means.

Perhaps it will be denied that any one proposes to trust instinct in the way I have described the cult here. It is true that no one does wholly trust it in practice, not even the most pagan of the anti-Puritans. Practice is often better than the theory. But I insist that this theory is central in our modern liberal culture, and that it has very serious consequences.

The most serious is that the theory undermines the intellectual resistance of those who see the evil of trying to run modern civilization on the notion that what happens to be interesting is, therefore, the measure of the public interest, and a guide to the conduct of the politician, the editor, the popular artist, and the teacher. In every one of the popular-

izing professions you will find among the ablest a
feeling of frustration and a vein of cynicism.   Their
pride of craft and their love of excellence encounter
not only the inevitable resistances which are part of
the game, but a certain moralized and highfalutin
doubt about whether it is not undemocratic, unpleas-
antly superior, and almost sinful to do what they
feel to be the first-rate thing.

They lack, in other words, the support of the
authoritative dogma of their time, the dogma of
instinct, when they seek the highest good.   It is as
if the intellect of mankind had conspired against
itself and had lamed its right arm in the eternal war
of light against darkness.   It is the business of
criticism to destroy this cult of the second best.
Destroying it will not, of course, insure the victory,
or suddenly transform the timid and timeserving—
the Burges and the Lubins—into courageous and
candid men.   But at least it will deprive the tempter
of his scripture when he whispers seductively in
men's ears that by drifting idly with the eddies of
popular interest they are serving the interests of
a free people.

July, 1922.

TO JUSTICE HOLMES ON HIS SEVENTY-FIFTH BIRTHDAY

THE country's business at Washington is conducted in an odor of dead and dying cigars suspended in steam heat. Out-of-doors Washington is widely planned and men might move about it thinking for a nation. But in the halls of Congress, in the committee rooms, the air is warm and foul. It drags upon you till you wilt and your head swims, and the faces of men testifying grow hazy. In that mean atmosphere, so like the corridor of a cheap hotel, there is an invitation to relax and grow bored and cease to care. You slouch in your seat, you dawdle through your business, compressed and dull and discouraged. Thick, tepid, tired air it is, in which visions die.

But there is at least one place in Washington where things have an altogether different quality, and no one, I think, comes away from it unmoved. It is the house of Mr. Justice Holmes. When you enter, it is as if you had come into the living stream of high romance. You meet the gay soldier who can talk of Falstaff and eternity in one breath, and tease the universe with a quip. "When I read absolute philosophy," he said once, "I feel as if I were sitting alone in a shadowy room. Every once in a while a mouse skips across the floor, and I catch glimpses of him as he darts into his hole. Then a wee voice seems to say, 'Lo! I am in the bosom of God.'" In him wisdom has lost its austerity and becomes a tumbling succession of imagery and laughter and outrage. There is always a window open to the night, but the perspective is that of the natural world. "I believe that we're in the belly of the universe, not that it is in us."

At seventy-five, a justice of the Supreme Court and a scholar known wherever the common law is studied, his heart is with the laughing sad men, who have mixed bitterness and beauty, and staked their souls on a gamble with life. He fought in the Civil War and was wounded; he has looked at death lightly, and known what it is to live dangerously. A sage with the bearing of a cavalier, his presence is an incitement to high risks for the sake of the enterprise and its memories. He wears wisdom like a gorgeous plume, and likes to stick the sanctities between the ribs.

He has lost nothing that young men have, and he has gained what a fine palate can take from the world. If it is true that one generation after another has depended upon its young to equip it with gayety and enthusiasm, it is no less true that each generation of the young depends upon those who have lived to illustrate what can be done with experience. They need to know that not all life withers in bad air. That is why young men feel themselves very close to Justice Holmes. He never fails to tell them what they want to hear, or to show them what they would wish men to be.

March 8, 1916.

AMERICANA LIBRARY

The City: The Hope of Democracy
By Frederic C. Howe
With a new introduction by Otis A. Pease

Bourbon Democracy of the Middle West, 1865-1896
By Horace Samuel Merrill
With a new introduction by the author

*The Deflation of American Ideals: An Ethical Guide
for New Dealers*
By Edgar Kemler
With a new introduction by Otis L. Graham, Jr.

Borah of Idaho
By Claudius O. Johnson
With a new introduction by the author

The Fight for Conservation
By Gifford Pinchot
With a new introduction by Gerald D. Nash

Upbuilders
By Lincoln Steffens
With a new introduction by Earl Pomeroy

The Progressive Movement
By Benjamin Parke De Witt
With a new introduction by Arthur Mann

*Coxey's Army: A Study of the
Industrial Army Movement of 1894*
By Donald L. McMurry
With a new introduction by John D. Hicks

Jack London and His Times: An Unconventional Biography
By Joan London
With a new introduction by the author

San Francisco's Literary Frontier
By Franklin Walker
With a new introduction by the author

Men of Destiny
By Walter Lippmann
With a new introduction by Richard Lowitt

Woman Suffrage and Politics:
The Inner Story of the Suffrage Movement
By Carrie Chapman Catt and Nettie H. Shuler
With a new introduction by T. A. Larson

The Dry Decade
By Charles Merz
With a new introduction by the author

The Conquest of Arid America
By William E. Smythe
With a new introduction by Lawrence B. Lee

The Territories and the United States, 1861–1890:
Studies in Colonial Administration
By Earl S. Pomeroy
With a new introduction by the author